Prepare to fly

Paragliding tips I wish I'd learned sooner

By Simon Blake

CONTENTS

This book is intended for the use of pilots who are about to pass, or have already passed their Club Pilot(Novice) certification in the UK, or its equivalent, and are wondering what they should do next. That is to say, people who have undergone a structured course of training under the supervision of a qualified instructor, demonstrated the necessary skills and attitude and passed the written exams in meteorology, theory of flight and air law that allow them to fly unsupervised within a club environment.

It's mainly aimed at those flying from hills, rather than tows, although there will inevitably be some crossover.

It is not intended to replace any part of the British Hang-gliding and Paragliding Association Pilot Handbook or other books about specific flying techniques such as launching, thermalling, cross country flying or weather assessment.

It is especially not intended to in any way replace instruction – there is relatively little in here about how to fly.

The subject of safety permeates all the advice herein. It may from time to time seem overcautious. Do not be put off, but resist the temptation to take shortcuts. Paragliding is amazing and enjoyable, but it is not forgiving of mistakes. Fly within your capabilities, and keep your estimates of your capabilities realistic.

A good general principle when learning is never to add more than one new factor at a time. If you buy or try something new, be it a wing, harness or just an instrument or camera, try them out for the first time at a site you know well, and in conditions that are well within your capabilities. If you're going to a new site, don't take or use anything that will distract you from the business of flying – use only the gear you're already completely comfortable with.

Seen on the wall of the bar at a sailplane club:

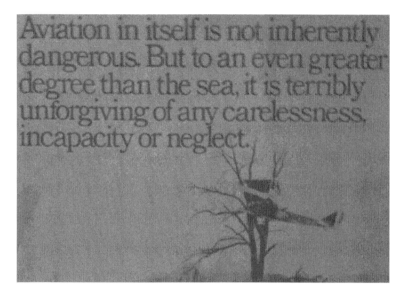

Aviation in itself is not inherently dangerous. But to an even greater degree than the sea, it is terribly unforgiving of any carelessness, incapacity or neglect.

Anyone who has been driving for a few years knows - your driving instructor did not teach you how to drive. Most of what you know about driving safely (assuming you drive safely...) you learn *after* passing your driving test. Your instructor's job was to equip you to pass the test and get from A to B without crashing, injuring or killing anyone.

Similarly, your paragliding instructor did not teach you to fly. If you have just passed your Club Pilot or equivalent rating, congratulations – you are now qualified to start learning to fly. This learning process will take a long time – in fact, it will never truly end. Becoming a pilot is a journey, not a destination. Fortunately, it's a really enjoyable journey that lasts as long as you like. Welcome!

Since getting my CP I've been flying off and on for seven years, but I still keenly remember the apprehension I felt when I first turned up to my local hill, red ribbon pinned to my harness, and pondered whether to fly or not.

I remember leafing through magazines with adverts for gear whose features and benefits I didn't understand, and spending money on things because I hadn't been flying for a while and shopping for paragliding kit was the best alternative available. I also remember gradually accumulating a collection of tips and tricks. This book is largely that collection.

When I first started, like a lot of pilots I kept a log, mainly for my own benefit. As I looked back through it there were nuggets in it that I wished I'd been told earlier. What follows is an attempt to allow newly qualified pilots to learn from my mistakes, and those of others.

One of the central messages of this book is that at all stages your learning can be made more efficient and your day more successful by doing proper preparation. There is relatively little in here concerned with what you need to be doing while in the air – if your instructor can't teach you to fly, a book certainly can't. Most of what I discuss and recommend is to do with those long hours *between* flights – when you're sitting on the hill or at home when you can't fly. If you make the right use of these times, you can learn more, more quickly than if you just blindly stumble forward when the weather's good, like I did.

For instance, your preparation for your next flight begins as soon as you're safely on the ground from your current one. Take care of the wing. Pack it neatly and carefully. This will not only extend its life and enhance its trade-in or resale value, it will also make your next flight easier because it will come out of the bag and inflate easily with the minimum of fuss and tangles. Inspect it as you pack it, making sure lines aren't knotted, twisted or looped randomly, and that the fabric is intact. If it's wet, make sure you air it out and get it dry before putting it away properly.

In general, time spent preparing will pay dividends on the hill in all sorts of situations. How much time you can dedicate to your preparation is up to you.

Paragliding is a sport that poses risk to life and limb. Every time you fly, you take personal responsibility for your decision to do so. ***"Taking off is optional. Landing is mandatory".*** If you're tired, or hungover, or nervous, or have any other reason that might compromise your flying – stay on the ground. Do some preparation for your next flight, so that next time, you will be ready.

PERSONAL LESSONS

Throughout this book, I'll be taking occasional timeouts to relate something that happened to me personally that taught me a lesson.

So far, the lessons I've had to learn in this way have been at worst inconvenient and occasionally a bit painful. I hope that by relating them here I can save you having to repeat them.

You will, of course, inevitably learn many such personal lessons of your own. If you make a mistake, no matter how serious or how trivial, don't beat yourself up about it. Don't forget it, either – use it. Think back over what you did, and what you could or should have done differently. Sometimes, the correct answer to this question is "I shouldn't have taken the glider out of the bag."

Ask the opinions of others, especially if there were witnesses. And when you've satisfied yourself that you understand where you went wrong, resolve not to do it again.

The best tool you can have for this progression is a notebook and pen. Get a ruled, spiral bound A5 notebook and pen, and keep them in your car. Every time you fly, fill it in. Do it before you drive home, while the memory of the flight is fresh. Record, as a minimum, the following:

- Date and time of day
- Weather and windspeed and direction – what it was when you arrived, and how it changed. This will enable to you spot patterns on how the weather develops, e.g. westerly winds tend to drop and turn

northerly, easterly winds stay consistent if they're strong, etc.

- Site visited
- Number of other aircraft present and types, e.g. five PG, one HG, two sailplanes, 1 R/C model
- Time spent in the air, and your cumulative hours to date.
- Number of takeoffs, reverse or forward, and an honest assessment of how well they went
- Number of slope landings, top landings, bottom landings, and an honest assessment of how well they went
- Anything specifically memorable about your flight – a close approach to a bird of prey, say, or a particularly good view or sunset – anything that will trigger recollection of it for you

Finally, at the bottom of every page, write "Today's Lesson".

Under that, be as honest as you can with yourself and write in something that you've done that you don't want to repeat. It doesn't need to be a big thing – the most trivial things can cause you problems you don't need. An example:

> *Personal Lesson: "Don't keep your great big keyring in your trouser pocket while flying". Now my keys are kept somewhere they won't dig into my thigh the whole time I'm in the air.*

Throughout this book, I've scattered a few more Personal Lessons. They are in each case the result of a "Today's

Lesson" note in my personal flying log. Please don't make the same mistakes I did.

A WORD ABOUT HOURS

"How many hours have you got?" is a common question. The BHPA recommends flying the red ribbon for ten hours after CP. Tricky sites are sometimes described as only being suitable for pilots with 20 hours after CP. But what is an hour?

Consider two pilots.

Newly CP-rated, the first turns up at his local sand dunes every day for a week. Every day for a week, there's a consistent, smooth, onshore breeze and nobody else flying. He takes off from the beach, soars back and forth for three hours listening to his iPod, never landing, never getting more than about a hundred feet up, chilled out and enjoying himself immensely, eventually lands anywhere he likes on the huge beach, and goes home. At the end of the week, he's got 20 hours in his book.

The second pilot lives inland near a usable ridge. She watches the weather reports and tries to get into the air whenever work and other commitments permit. The site is small and crowded, so she does a good deal of waiting and talking to other pilots. She also does a good deal of ground handling while she waits for the airspace to be a bit emptier, with a local club coach looking on. It's a hard walk up, so she's strongly motivated to learn to top land and side land, and practices doing these things a lot. She rarely flies for more than five or ten minutes at a stretch, because she's constantly practicing her slope or top landings, and in any case the novel mental strain of watching out for the other pilots and keeping an eye on the changing weather means she doesn't want to be up amongst it for too long at one go. When it's time to go home, she's required to hit a reasonably restricted landing field which has trees along one edge and is out of sight of takeoff. If she's lucky, and dedicated, in two or three months she'll get 20 hours airtime.

Of these two pilots, who would you rather share airspace with? Who would cope best with a new site? They've both got the same number of hours...

The point here is that hours are a very crude measure of your experience, especially early on. In training, you may never have flown for more than five or ten minutes straight. When you find yourself able to stay in the air for half an hour or more at a stretch, with nobody on the radio saying "Land now", the novelty and the temptation to simply stay in the air at any cost for as long as possible can be irresistible. I'm not saying you shouldn't do it, because we are after all here to fly. Furthermore, as your skills develop, the ability to remain comfortable and alert and fly for hours at a stretch is something you will need to learn if you want to fly long distances cross country. Before you do that, however, you need to practice ground handling, take offs and landings far more than the few you needed for your CP.

Personal Lesson: Shortly after I got my CP, I had a single flight lasting over three hours. At the time, that one flight represented something like 60% of my total flying hours. It was great, but six flights of half an hour each, with some top landings in between, would have taught me far more.

Don't be too concerned, early on, about just getting your raw number of hours up. There is no UK hours league competition, and a red ribbon isn't something you should be rushing to throw away.

If you have an incident, or even a near miss, it can be quite embarrassing. You may think "only I could be so daft". You are almost certainly completely wrong about that.

As the representative body for the sport in the UK, the BHPA collects and compiles incident statistics. They can only do this with the cooperation of UK pilots.

If there is a deficiency in a particular piece of equipment, or something lacking in some element of training being given by a particular instructor, or school, or all schools, then those faults may give rise to a regular pattern of incidents. If someone spots that pattern, the cause can be traced and action can be taken to address the problem.

Those patterns can only be spotted if incidents *and near misses* get reported.

So if you're injured, even slightly, narrowly escape injury, notice some manufacturing defect in your equipment, or even have a near miss that doesn't result in any damage, but could have, then get it reported. Nobody will think any less of you, and your report may form part of a pattern that results in life-saving action being taken.

Incident reporting forms can be downloaded from the BHPA website. www.bhpa.co.uk/pdf/IR.pdf

The first stage of preparation is having the right equipment. If you have the right equipment, set up correctly, your flying time will be more pleasurable and less stressful, and you can focus on learning stuff.

WING SELECTION

A common question from the soon-to-qualify or recently qualified is "Which wing should I buy?" This is sometimes followed by something along the lines of "My instructor says I'm pretty good, so I don't want a beginner's wing…" Here's my take on that.

Beginner wings are designed to look after you. That is, as they fly along, if they encounter mild turbulence like the edge of a thermal or a bit of rotor, their angle of attack tends not to change much compared to a "hotter" wing. They fly quite "solidly". This is reassuring to the novice. They don't convey much information to the pilot about what the air is doing, and they don't require much input to stay in shape. They tend to resist collapse, and when they do collapse, they usually recover quickly and benignly, often before the pilot has even realised there's a problem. Under almost all circumstances if there's a problem with the wing, the best thing the pilot can do is put their hands up and let it start flying again. Only if it's not sorted itself out after a few seconds should the pilot begin making efforts to help. The cost for this relative security is lower speed, a poorer climb rate and poorer glide ratio than higher-rated wings. The differences, however, are actually pretty small, and most modern "beginner" wings have performance that comparable to competition wings of the 1990s. It's perfectly possible to catch thermals, reach cloudbase and fly a proper cross country flight on an EN A wing.

Higher performance comes at a cost of stability. "Better" wings will fly slightly faster, but won't be as stable in pitch. They will tell the pilot what's going on, but they will conversely require the pilot to actively control them more – far more in some cases. Note the word "actively" does not mean "consciously" – the aim is that our control of the glider should be entirely subconscious. When you're riding a bicycle, you don't need *consciously* to think about the business of balancing it or pedalling, but you do *actively* balance as you ride along – you're not just a passenger. The action of balancing is entirely instinctive – you don't need to think about it.

YOUR FIRST SOLO FLIGHTS

When you first turn up to a hill on your own, it can be a nervous experience. If you learned abroad or somewhere other than near your home, your local hill may be a site you've never flown or perhaps even seen before, and now you're here, all alone. Is the wind strong enough? Too strong? The right direction, or too far off the hill? Is there a designated landing field, and can you make it there from here? Could you top land if you need to? How about a slope landing? Let's say you manage to unpack your crispy new wing alone for the very first time, get it checked, inflated and over your head without incident.

Now you need to do your very first ever unsupervised launch. You need to make sure you're clear of the terrain and the wing is flying OK, and then get back into the seat. If it's anything like a decent day for flying, there are most likely other gliders in the air – you need to be watching where they all are. Depending on the site, you may be sharing the air with two or twenty other paragliders, speedwings, hang-gliders, sail-planes or R/C models, or any mixture of the above. You may have bought some fancy instruments and attached them to some sort of cockpit, either integral to a sleek pod harness or a separate unit slung somewhere across your lap, or just strapped round your leg. They may or may not work correctly, and even if they work they may, or may not hang in a position where you can see them. You might have a camera or some kind of high-def digital action camcorder on your helmet, lap, or wing, along with a remote control to start and stop filming.

You'll be trying to find the best bit of lift. You will (or should be) experimenting with different ways of turning (more weightshift or less? Weight first then brake, or the other way round, or somewhere in between? How much brake travel, and how fast? When I hit lift, how long do I wait to turn? Etc.). You will be wondering why your instrument is reading out in metres instead of feet, or what the noise it just made means, or why it seems to be pointing towards a waypoint programmed in by the previous owner, or where the hell that bloke on the blue wing has gone who you're sure was just above and behind you a few seconds ago. Your left leg is being pinched by the strap which is too tight, whereas your right leg strap feels like it's undone. Are you sure you fastened it properly?

Now... with all of these things competing for your attention, do you want to be flying a wing that requires you to *think*? I'd say no.

One day, you will be prepared – you'll know the site well, your equipment will be packed right, you'll know how to operate everything, you'll know a few of the local pilots and recognise their wings, and the sense of where people are in the air will come naturally. Your turns will be smooth and fluid and instinctive, your instruments will tell you what you want to know and nothing more, and you'll sit back into your harness after launch comfortably and confidently. Your conscious mind will be free of distractions and you can focus on flying. You will be, in short, a pilot, not a passenger. When you've reached this point, and not before, you're ready for a wing you need to think about flying… and then you'll have some more learning to do.

But for your first hours post-qualification, stick firmly to an EN A or low-end EN B wing that will look after you and forgive you for occasionally being a bit of a passenger while you learn to do all the many other things a pilot has to do.

As to the exact wing, don't worry much about the choice. All the major manufacturers' wings are, nowadays, worth flying, so choice mainly comes down to colour, price, availability, and any personal recommendations. If your instructor wants to sell you a package which includes a major manufacturer's EN A or low-end EN B wing, take their advice.

WEIGHT RANGES

One factor that should significantly influence your choice is weight range – gliders are certified between a maximum and minimum weight, and they perform best when the pilot and *all* their gear is somewhere near or just above the middle of that range.

When picking a wing, don't forget that your "all up" weight is yourself, your boots, helmet, gloves, wing and harness (including reserve), PLUS all the other stuff you'll inevitably accumulate. Factor in your lunch, a litre or two to drink, instruments, a jacket and some other stuff, and your all up weight might easily be five or even ten kgs more than you initially considered.

You may think, fine, I'll just get the next size up. For instance, your preferred glider might be certified as a Medium at 85-105kg, and you're tipping the scales at 103kg. But add on your lunch and a couple of litres of water and you're over the certified weight.

So you might think you simply need the Large size, certified at 100-120kg. That'll be nice and floaty on light days, but if it gets rough or strong at all the much reduced loading will mean the wing is more prone to collapse and less responsive.

A preferable alternative if you find yourself in this position would be to look at a different wing altogether, perhaps from another manufacturer where the weight range is, say, 90-110kg. Now you're comfortably in the middle, with some wiggle room to add lunch, radios, cameras or whatever and still be flying well-loaded and certified.

RESERVE PARACHUTE

Reserve parachutes are available second hand, at much more reasonable prices than a new one.

Think about that for a moment.

When you reach for your reserve, it's because everything you've tried has failed. Your glider is no longer flying, you are heading at the hard ground or deadly water at speed and you have just one last chance at living through the next minute. At that point, as you reach for that handle, the fact that you cunningly saved a couple of hundred quid three years ago by getting a second hand reserve will not be a comfort.

Buy a new one. Even if all your other gear is second hand, do not skimp on the reserve parachute or its fitting and packing. It is your last chance. There is no greater exemplar of the phrase "false economy" than a cheap parachute.

Get the right size – the BHPA have published guidelines on maximum advisable descent rates. There is a school of thought that says smaller chutes open faster, but the difference is measured in tenths of a second, whereas differences in descent rate can be the difference between an ankle sprain and a broken leg or worse.

Steerable reserves are available, but they add complication to a system which, at this stage, you want to be as simple as possible. A lightweight reserve of the right size is fine, but you will find that to halve the weight you have to double the cost.

Finally, don't just fit it and forget it. Get it repacked at the recommended intervals, and if you can, attend an organised repack so that you can practice throwing it and see what's in the bag and how it's packed. For many pilots the contents of the bag under their seat is a mystery they never think about. If you at least watch it being packed, it will dispel some of the mystery and increase your confidence in the system.

Your harness is, in many ways, a more important choice than your wing, not least because it will most probably last you a good deal longer. While you will sooner or later upgrade your wing for a newer, higher performance model, your harness could easily see you through three or four wings. Like the driver's seat of your car, you're going to be spending a lot of hours sitting in it, so make sure you're going to like being there.

There are a bewildering array of harnesses available, and much of the available printed advice about them is out of date, with references to "cross bracing" and other relics of a bygone era.

The most important things to consider when choosing a harness are comfort, protection and weight. It is vitally important that you get a harness that is the right size and a comfortable fit for you. Buying a cheap one that's slightly too large or small or a bit heavy is a false economy – you may be carrying the thing a long way, most of it uphill, and how well it fits is directly related to how well you will fly with it. The harness is your connection to the wings you will own. Take some time to get the right one.

One feature to look for in any harness you buy of whatever type is the relatively recent development of the "safe T-bar" style of fastening. Deaths have been caused in the past by pilots taking off with only their chest strap fastened, so that when they launch, they slide down out of their seat and are left hanging from their armpits with no control over the glider, until they sooner or later fall out, usually to their death. The Safe-T-bar style of buckle simply connects the chest strap to the leg straps, and means that if you've got

20

anything fastened at all, you should be safe. It's not foolproof, but it's a big improvement on completely separate straps.

The choice ultimately breaks down to one of four types, in order of increasing weight:

1. Lightweight mountain harness
2. Reversible harness
3. Standard/open/recreational harness
4. Pod harness

Until you've got a reasonable degree of experience, you shouldn't even think about types 1 or 4.

Lightweight mountain harnesses are minimalist scraps of fabric with little or no protection against bumps. Realistically you are going to get dragged around a bit before you get your ground handling dialled, so you're going to need a bit of protection. Mountain harnesses also usually have no place to stash a reserve parachute, since the pilots flying them often fly without one, or mount it in front of them. Since you are definitely going to be flying with a reserve, the extra complication, hassle and expense of flying with a front mount is something you can do without for now.

Pod harnesses look great in the air, and are increasingly popular because they're comfortable, warm, and are getting lighter and easier to carry. They also offer very slightly higher performance when gliding between thermals due to their aerodynamic shape, although for a good pilot on a good wing, it's perfectly possible to fly a hundred miles in Britain without using a pod. They are, however, still heavier than some alternatives, and require a good deal more setting up and fiddling with than a standard harness. There are also legitimate safety concerns regarding pilots getting airborne in pods without having fastened their leg straps, and the effect of being in a pod during a collapse. Save the pod for later in your career.

So as a beginner, your choice comes down to standard, or reversible.

STANDARD HARNESSES

The standard harness is the conventional, popular choice. It's very important that you buy the right size, so buying unseen off the internet is not recommended. You should be able to sit in the harness you're buying before you pay. Ideally, sit in at least a couple for comparison.

Unlike wings, for which it's often possible to arrange an extended demo period, dealers generally won't lend you a harness to try out, so unless you can borrow one off a buddy, your choice will come down to what feels right when it's hanging in the shop. Sit down into it and play with all the straps. Make sure you can adjust your seating position – you should be able to set it to keep you quite upright, or allow you to lie quite far back, and anywhere in between.

Can you reach the reserve handle easily? Is there room in the back pocket for your rucksack and all the other stuff you'll bring to the hill? How comfortable is it to walk around in when the back is full of stuff and you're clipped in? (You're going to be carrying your balled up glider around a good deal when you fail to stay up, so you want that to be as little effort as possible) And most important, is it comfortable and the right size, or are you pinched or slopping around in it?

Try to connect a speed bar and push it to its full extent and see how that changes how the seat feels. When the time comes that you need to push full bar for five or ten minutes straight, or longer, you don't want the action to turn your chair into a torture device.

Back protection in standard harnesses generally comes in two types – airbag or foam.

In an airbag harness, a large cavity within the harness fills with air through a one-way valve, and acts as a cushion in the event of impact. The advantage is obvious – if your protection is a bag of air, its weight is negligible. The disadvantage is that you're depending on the valve-flap to retain the air, which means you need to look after it and make sure it doesn't get bent or otherwise damaged. You've also got next to no protection until the bag has inflated, which it generally does once you've flown forward a few feet. This obviously leaves you vulnerable in those moments when you're still on or close to the ground, the times you, as a novice, might need protection the most.

Foam protectors are there all the time, and will protect you somewhat even if you're dragged by a half-inflated wing before you've got off the ground. The penalty is obviously weight and size, making them a little harder to fit into the rucksack with your glider.

REVERSIBLE HARNESSES

Reversible harnesses are the other option you should consider. These are harnesses which turn inside out to form a rucksack for carrying your glider up the hill. They are almost invariably airbag rather than foam protected, and thus are light by harness standards, and given that you won't need a separate rucksack, that's another kilogramme or more you can save. A lighter pack means an easier walk, which can mean you're more motivated to walk up, which can mean you'll fly more and learn faster. Reversible harnesses have their disadvantages too, however, beyond what's already been said about airbag protection. Ultimately, a reversible harness is unlikely to be quite as durable as a conventional model, and if there's a problem with your rucksack – a busted zip, say, that needs replacing – it affects the harness, and vice versa. Abrasion to the rucksack material can mean abrasion to the airbag material, which reduces its effectiveness. They're also not cheap, typically costing ten or twenty per cent more than a comparable standard harness.

Take your time to get your choice of harness right, and it will greatly increase your flying pleasure and the rate you learn.

Once you've selected a harness, don't just pay and take it home. Take some time in the shop to get it set up before you leave. A shop selling harnesses should be able to hang it so that you can sit in it.

Attach and adjust the speed system and stirrup (see later), and adjust and test every strap and buckle you can find. Having tested the full range of adjustment, get your seat position set up so that you're comfortable. Most importantly, find out the recommended chest strap setting for your glider and your weight, and set it correctly in the shop. If possible, lock it in that position, or at least mark it so it's obvious.

When you're done setting up the harness, and if there's space in the shop, get your wing out and attach the risers to the carabiners. Attach the speed bar brummel hooks, and check the operation of the speed system. Finally, pack your glider and harness away, and see that you can fit everything in with a bit of room to spare.

The shop should have someone who can fit your reserve parachute into the harness for you. If they do, ask nicely if, once they've packed it, you can do a practice throw. This will give you the confidence that if you pull that handle it will at least come out of the bag as per design. Get them to show you what a properly set up reserve should look like on your harness. Take a photo of it with your phone.

If the shop can't fit your reserve, make sure it's fitted by a certified repacker. Don't try to do it yourself.

Ideally, you should walk out of the shop with your new harness and glider neatly packed, set up and ready to fly, needing no further adjustment. This may take some time, but an hour spent at this point really can save you hours of frustration later, and you're spending hundreds, possibly thousands with that dealer. Obviously you can do all this at home, but help from someone who knows what they're doing is invaluable.

Gloves are an underrated piece of equipment. I'm frequently amazed to see people flying with bare hands. Don't be one of those people. Your gloves should have leather palms and fingers. They're not there primarily to protect you from the cold, they're to protect you from your glider lines (or someone else's).

You should have your gloves on *before you take the glider out* of its concertina bag or stuff sack. This way, if it tries to take a trip across the hill without your permission, you can simply grab a line, and it will flag out and everything will be fine. Try that without gloves, or with thin fabric gloves, and you could be in pain for weeks. Hold a single paraglider line with an ungloved hand and when the wing is loaded, the line will cut through your flesh like a wire through cheese, and it's not a wound that heals easily. **Always wear your gloves when the glider is open to the wind**.

> *Personal lesson: my glider took an unscheduled trip across the hill which I was able to bring under control with my ungloved hand. I still have the scars on two fingers. Get your gloves on before you get the wing out.*

Never fly without a helmet. There is a theory that passive safety measures encourage an attitude of complacency about risk. This is fine in theory, but in practice it's possible, even probable, that you're going to get dragged across the ground at least once, no matter how carefully you practice. Any boxer will tell you it doesn't take much of an impact on your unprotected head to really ruin your day, or your life, so wear a helmet. Wear one that's certified for paragliding to EN966 standard, and when it's over five years old, throw it away and get a new one.

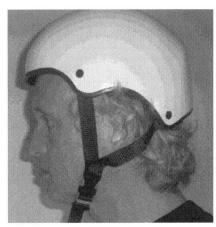

Teardrop-shaped aerodynamic helmets with chinguards look the business, but for the beginner, less is more. In particular, it can help a lot to have your ears uncovered. You're more connected to the elements, and also if you're using a radio earpiece it's easier to relocate it if it falls out. A simple open face helmet is therefore recommended. Avoid those ones that have a sort of fin-shaped spoiler profile at the back – imagine the effect on your neck if your head was knocked back. Unless you're in an international standard competition flying a top-end prototype glider in a streamlined pod on full speedbar, how aerodynamic your head is will make absolutely no difference at all.

Finally on helmets: helmet on first, then clip in to your harness. Unclip *fully* first, then helmet off. **You should never, ever, be clipped into your harness without your helmet on**. If you ever catch yourself clipped in without your helmet on, give yourself a good hard talking to and don't do it again. This is true even if, indeed especially if, you're "just" ground handling. The ground is the thing you're going to hit your head on. If you're not in a position to simply let go of the glider and let it blow away without you – make sure your helmet is on and fastened.

> *Personal lesson: Flying a benign coastal site, low dunes, in a smooth wind, I stopped for a rest. Ready to go again, I wing-walked the glider up the dune. I was at this point just ground handling, and in pretty easy conditions. I stumbled slightly, which unbalanced the wing, which dragged me no more than ten yards across the marram grass, during which I took good thump to the head from a hidden rock. I was fine – but only because I had my helmet on. I was very grateful for it.*

Flying boots with flaps protecting the lacing hooks are good, but a decent pair of hiking boots with good ankle protection and, if you like, a pair of gaiters over them to cover the laces are probably OK.

You've got your wing, your harness and your reserve. You've got a helmet and a decent pair of gloves. You've some warm clothing and some hiking boots. What other equipment do you need?

None, really.

Seriously – you should be doing a lot of ground handling and a bit of ridge soaring, and if it's not too strong, having a go at thermalling when you get the chance. For this you will not really need anything more than the stuff in the paragraph above.

But it's winter time or you've just got five numbers on the lottery or you've just nothing better to do and you want to buy some toys. What do you *want*?

STIRRUP

A stirrup is simply a solid bar on a pair of cords that connects to your carabiners and threads down to the seat of your harness. It gives you somewhere to put your feet when you're flying so that you adopt a more comfortable and aerodynamic supine posture, rather than just having your legs dangling down. Sitting like this helps you weight shift more effectively, and it helps you get into the seat immediately after launch with the minimum of fuss and risk.

Pound for pound, a stirrup can probably do more to improve the way you fly than any other single piece of gear. Buy one when you buy your harness, and get it set up correctly in the shop. When you're comfortably positioned in the seat, extend your legs straight out to the front. The stirrup bar should be adjusted so that it's nestled firmly in the crook of the heel of your boots, so that you can push yourself into the seat.

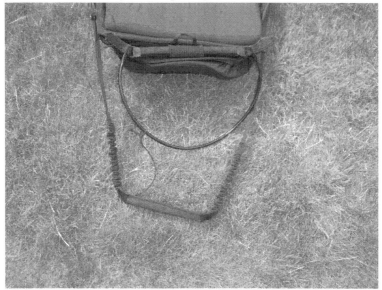

Tie the first step of your speed system to the corner of your stirrup with a piece of elastic shock cord, and the speed bar will always be accessible and easy to reach without looking for it.

There've been too many accidents caused by pilots either pulling down the brakes while trying to push themselves into their seats, or taking their hands off the controls and losing concentration while they try to get back into their seat the moment they're off the ground. A stirrup means you can retain full control of the glider at all times and get into the seat without a problem.

Using a stirrup may take a little practice. When you've laid out your glider and you're just about to pick up the harness and put it on, first step through the stirrup with just one foot – let's say the left.

When you put the harness on, the bar should now be hanging in front of and slightly below your left knee. It shouldn't be in the way.

Do your launch, forward or reverse, as normal.

Once you're safely in the air, simply raise the bar with your left shin and put your right foot into it and push.

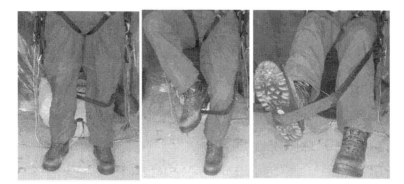

You'll slot back comfortably into the seat of your harness – no wriggling, no taking your hands off the controls to push or pull on straps, just a single smooth movement and you're back into the seat and flying off.

Weight shift can be achieved by pushing with one foot and slightly bending the other knee. You can be quite subtle with it.

Hold the stirrup forward with one foot and reach back with the other, and if you've followed the shock cord tip above you'll be able to push the speed bar without ever looking at it or having to mess about trying to move it to your boot with your hand.

Find some way of hanging your harness up at home, and practice this.

When training, your day may usually consist of quite short flights interspersed with walks back up the hill. For this, normal outdoor gear such as windproof fleece jacket over a base layer and sturdy trousers are fine.

However, as your flying improves and becomes more frequent, things change. You will spend less time walking back up the hill. You may spend a long time parawaiting. And when you eventually get off the hill, instead of being tense and nervous on a three minute sled ride, you'll be more relaxed, and possibly flying quite high and for an hour or more at a time. All of these things will mean you could easily get very cold indeed. Be prepared for this.

Of course, you can easily continue simply to dress in normal outdoor gear, and just add layers to take account of the cold.

A proper flying suit, however, offers some advantages. It's a dedicated bit of kit, so it can live in your glider bag. If it's in there, you can in theory turn up to the hill dressed in more or less anything and pull your flying suit on over it and be fine. Lacking any opening at the waist, a one piece suit can be a good deal warmer than separate jacket and trousers of equivalent thickness.

Suits typically feature fabric loops on the legs designed to make sure that a leg strap for your instrument stays where it's supposed to. They also have convenient pockets for stashing your radio, and full length zips to make them easy to put on and take off. They can protect your civilian clothes from the sheep poo or worse that you might find in the landing field, and your skin from the dragging you might get across rocky terrain.

34

There are those who ridicule the use of flying suits, considering them fit only for dorks. I can understand this attitude to a certain extent, but for me the comfort and convenience of a suit I can keep in my glider bag outweighs any fashion crime I might be committing by wearing one.

COMPASS

As a beginner, this should ideally be the first "instrument" you buy. It's cheap, it doesn't need batteries, it doesn't have any buttons you need to press, and you'll hardly ever need to look at it. See the later section on cloud flying for details on why you'll need it and how to use it.

For now, buy a simple, cheap ball compass of the type you fit to your car dashboard, and fit it to your harness. Make sure you fix it somewhere that it's not near anything magnetic! Don't use a Silva compass or similar hiker's type – they need to be kept flat, and when it's time to use it, you will want it to just work without faff. Also don't bother buying an expensive back-bearing compass with rotating bezel marked at degree intervals. You won't be navigating with your compass, you'll be using it roughly in an emergency – see later on. Keep it simple and cheap.

INSTRUMENTS

The most visible and desirable gadgets the average experienced pilot you see on the hill is packing are those beeping electronic devices in their laps. There's a much larger discussion of these things later on, but for now here are three quick points:

- You really honestly don't need one at all yet.

35

- When you do get one, don't waste your time and money on one that doesn't have GPS – i.e. don't buy something that's just a vario
- No single gadget will do everything you will eventually need

RADIO

Legally, in order to transmit radio from any aircraft, one should use a properly licenced airband radio operated by a trained operator. This is the official position, and if you want to talk to air traffic control, by all means take the time and make the effort to get certified to do so. You will, however, find almost no other paraglider pilots in the UK to talk to.

Meanwhile, many paraglider pilots legally own and illegally operate 2m radio sets while flying. So long as you stick to a certain very narrow range of frequencies (143.950MHz is popular) which don't interfere with anyone else, this usage has historically been tolerated, and there is no reason to think that this situation should not continue.

Many dealers will sell you a radio such as Yaesu or Alinco for upwards of £100. Alternatively, you can go to an online auction site, find a Chinese-made radio like the Puxing PX-777 for half that price or less, and "Buy It Now". This is a popular choice.

HEADSETS

Your radio should be firmly attached to, or stashed inside, your gear or clothing. In order to transmit, you're going to need either a handset or a headset. There are a huge variety of these devices available at wildly varying prices.

The first and most important thing to know about headsets of any kind is the importance of NOT transmitting. If you're transmitting, everyone else within range on that channel can hear you, and they can't speak while you're talking. When you're high in the air, even a cheap radio can transmit clearly over a hundred miles, so that could be a lot of people. If you're saying something brief and sensible, like "Derek, I'm in a climb over here" or "Sue, I'm down and safe, you get as far as you can and I'll come get you in the car," few will mind overhearing you. If you chatter inanely and at length, it might be annoying for them, but it's tolerable. Try not to, though.

The ultimate sin with a radio is simply transmitting noise, or worse still, the repetitive beep of a vario and nothing else, for hours because you're keying your mike and don't realise it. For this reason, headset selection is very important.

First and foremost, do not under any circumstances buy a voice-activated headset. "Voice activated" actually means "noise activated", which for paragliding purposes means "wind noise activated", which means "will transmit all the time". Don't buy one.

What you want is a handset or a PTT (Push To Talk) headset, with a button on a cord. You can mount the button somewhere on your harness, stick some Velcro to it and attach it to your glove or chest, or simply thread it down your sleeve and leave it dangling by your hand. Whatever you do with it, make sure that you can't push it by accident while flying or ground handling, otherwise you'll be keying the mike repeatedly when you don't need to.

Personal lesson: On my longest ever
XC flight I was in a sky full of fifty or

sixty other pilots, many of them on radio, and one oblivious person (not me) was transmitting the noise of the wind and their vario for the better part of an hour. If you hear people complaining about someone keying their mike, but you can't hear it happening – it's you. Don't be that person.

Sets come in three basic types:

1. Handset
2. Throat mike
3. Earpiece mike

HANDSET

A handset is just what it sounds like – a small handheld mike/speaker set with the PTT on the side that connects to the radio usually with a coiled cable. You can clip or Velcro it somewhere convenient, and they're pretty robust, easy to use and foolproof.

The downside of the handset is that you need a hand fully off the controls to operate it, and you may need to hold it to your mouth while you speak. As long as you're sensible and only speak when you're in smooth air, this shouldn't be too much of an issue.

THROAT MIKE

Throat mikes eliminate the issue of wind noise by picking up the vibrations of your neck directly. They come connected to an earpiece, often via a transparent tube, so you can hear conversations. They're often used by people such as store detectives because you can put the PTT in your pocket, the transparent earpiece in your ear, and speak very quietly and still be heard, all the while not looking like you're even carrying a radio. My experience is that for active sports like paragliding, where your head is (or should be) constantly swivelling round, they don't stay in place very well. They can be got pretty cheaply, though, so they may be worth trying.

EARPIECE MIKE

The earpiece mike is what it sounds like – you just stick it in your ear and it's a combined speaker and microphone, picking up the vibrations from your head and transmitting your voice. It's similarly free of wind noise but more tolerant of movement than the throat mike. Again, they're available pretty cheaply. This is my preferred style of radio headset, but the choice is a very personal one.

If you fly with one instrument, you can strap it to your thigh. The loops on your flying suit will keep it in place. Soon, though, you'll collect enough gadgets that strapping them to your leg is impractical. At this point, or possibly before, you'll want a cockpit.

This is simply a bag that keeps all your stuff in one place, and mounts your instruments together, conveniently visible and usable in flight.

The big advantage with having a cockpit is that all your "stuff" – food, drink, instruments, radio, camera, airmaps, etc. – is in one place. If you've prepared properly, you can stuff the cockpit in your glider bag safe in the knowledge that everything you need is in there.

Cockpits are often fitted with an array of straps and buckles, and it can be far from obvious how to actually attach the damn thing to yourself the first few times out. Your preparation should include hanging your harness up somewhere, sitting in it, and experimenting with how to attach your cockpit. You absolutely should NOT just clip it on, take off, then attempt to fiddle with it while flying.

In general, there'll be a couple of straps at either side near the top. These should go through your carabiners, rather than any part of the harness. There may also be some other straps, perhaps elasticated, that can thread through your legs straps to make the thing sit up straight if it doesn't already. If your cockpit isn't sitting right and you can't see your instruments, you have two sensible options. You can either ignore it – your vario will still beep even if you can't see it – or you can land and sort it out. Messing about with it in the air is a very bad idea. Prepare: learn the best way of fitting your cockpit by testing it at home, then stick with that method.

CONCERTINA BAG

Your glider will likely have been supplied with a stuff sack and a couple of compression straps, using which it's perfectly possible to pack it using any number of folding techniques, or indeed simply stuffing it in.

However, modern gliders have mylar panels, or increasingly commonly nylon rods, reinforcing and shaping the leading edge and defining the cell openings. Some even have semi-rigid reinforcement on the trailing edge too. Remember, preparation for your next flight begins as soon as you and your wing are safely on the ground after this one, and time spent packing your glider carefully can make it last longer and be worth more when it comes time to sell it or trade it in. More immediately, just a few extra minutes spent packing it right will save time unpacking it next time you fly.

Many manufacturers recommend that their gliders are packed "concertina" style, which is to say with the leading edge protection gathered together and kept neatly flat, and the trailing edge folded in a zigzag pattern working up the wing chord. This is all very well if you're packing a wing on a perfectly smooth, flat floor indoors, as one manufacturer's Youtube video demonstration shows. Doing the job in a windy field full of thistles or on a rocky beach in a sea breeze is a different business.

A concertina bag can make the packing process much easier. It's simply a tube of material with clips or a zip, and some straps at one end to keep your gathered leading edge neat

41

and flat and together. The idea is you lay the bag down, dump the wing on top, and gather up the leading edge. Once it's together, you clip it up, and then just zip up the sausage shaped bag, stuffing the glider in as you go. It can make packing very much easier, particularly if it's windy. It's also worth saying that it can make UNpacking much easier too, because a well concertina packed wing comes out of the bag very neat. If there's any kind of wind on the hill, you need only open out the middle half dozen cells of the glider, give the A risers a pull, and the wing will inflate and unfold itself out to the tips like a magic trick. This does take some practice, but once you've got it to work it's a revelation.

There are three types of concertina bag, and the difference does matter.

Some models have zips that start at the leading edge. This does make them quite easy to use, because that's the end you've already gathered together. However, as you zip the bag shut, you're forcing air towards the trailing edge, where it doesn't have any way of escaping except through the cloth. Ideally, you wouldn't want to force air through the cloth, as porosity is bad for glider material. It's not a huge concern, but there is an alternative.

Other models have the zip starting at the trailing edge. The gathered leading edge is strapped in, then you start pulling in and zipping up from the other end. This is slightly more fiddly, but it does mean the trapped air is forced towards the cell openings where it can escape more easily without having to pass through the glider cloth.

Lightweight concertina bags without zips simply have clip fasteners at intervals along their length. This obviously allows you to start wherever you like, but is a tiny bit fiddlier than using a zip.

Overall, a concertina bag is an excellent piece of kit and well worth investing in.

CAMERAS

Facebook, Youtube, Vimeo and Flickr, and many other online services, have made sharing photos and videos ridiculously easy. Rapid advances in technology mean that you can now buy cameras and video cameras of unprecedented quality for reasonable prices, and edit the films you produce on even quite a basic PC or Mac.

Paragliding is of course a particularly photogenic sport, with the bright colours of the wings against the blue of the sky and the fluffy clouds, and the new perspective one gets with an aerial view.

There will be some more detailed discussion later on about cameras, camcorders, and making videos but for now, I repeat the advice given earlier regarding wing selection: give yourself as few distractions as possible. Don't start thinking about in-flight photography or filming until you're 100% confident and comfortable with your flying. Even then, be careful.

It's also worth passing on some advice re: helmet cams. It is quite easy, if you're getting dragged and tumbled along the ground, to have a line catch on one of your harness buckles, your boot or similar. This can make regaining some control difficult or impossible until you're untangled. A helmet cam turns your head from a nice, smooth ball with no readily line-grabbing crevices into pointy device which could have been designed specifically for causing problems. This is a particular concern during the turning-round part of a reverse launch, when the twisted lines have to untwist above your head in exactly the space now occupied by a camera. It is particularly unpleasant having a fully-loaded paraglider line trying to twist your head off.

If you must mount a camera on your helmet, try to do it with Velcro, and use a secondary attachment, i.e. a lanyard, in case it comes off.

MISCELLANEOUS OTHER GEAR

There are a few other bits of kit you'd be as well to have stashed somewhere in your glider bag which you can pick up as you go along.

Small rolltop dry bag: these things are available from any hiking gear shop. As with the cockpit, if you're prepared properly, you can grab it and know that all your miscellaneous stuff in together in one place.

Toilet paper: light and indispensible. Don't leave home without it, and if you have to use it, do so responsibly. Glad to say I don't have a personal lesson to relate about the time I forgot this.

Drinking system: bladder and tube arrangements that allow you to drink while flying are brilliant. Do, however, make sure you get a bite valve that can be locked closed. And lock it closed.

Personal lesson

It's a beautiful warm sunny day at my local hill, and I've been flying happily back and forth for some time, taking the occasional sip from my drinking tube. I've top landed for a rest, but now I'm ready to go again. The wing is up above my head, and I'm looking up at it, playing with it a bit before I take off. I become aware of a cool, damp sensation in my groinal area. Not good. I look down, and my flying suit looks like I've enthusiastically wet myself. This is bad enough, but then I realise what I've done. My drinking tube has dangled down my chest, and as I'm ground handling the wing, my cockpit, and specifically my expensive GPS/vario, has pressed up against the bite valve. I've emptied about half a pint of water into my instrument. It made a few more plaintive beeps for about five minutes, and then died. I still fly with a drinking tube, but I secure it high on my harness strap and always, always, lock the valve when I'm done drinking.

Blister plasters: if you've got a long walk in to your local hill, or if you might face a long walk out of an XC, pack some of these.

Airmap(s): buy a 1:500,000 airmap of your area and put it in your bag. You're legally required to carry one if you go XC, and even if you think that's a long way in your future, you can get it out and study it while you wait for the wind to drop/get stronger/change direction.

Buff: it can get proper cold up there!

Sunglasses: if you wear polarised sunglasses, check you can still read your instruments. Flying on a sunny day without sunglasses can be a bit wearing. Do make sure you get proper UV protecting ones – on a decent day's flying you'll be out in the sun quite a bit. Don't buy expensive ones, though – you'll inevitably crush them in your bag or sit on them at some stage.

Insect repellent: depending where you fly, this might be absolutely vital.

Sunblock: even in England you can get sunburn, especially on high pressure windless days when you're just sitting around hatless waiting for the wind to start.

Hook knife: you never know.

MP3 player: can make solo walk-ups pass easier. Music or podcasts can take your mind off the slog. I recommend the Friday Night Comedy podcast from Radio 4, and The Bugle. I strongly advise against listening to an iPod while flying, however. This is very much a personal preference based on one or two experiences, but I feel it's far better to be able to hear the breeze.

Jelly babies. Easy to eat even while flying for a quick sugar boost.

Laminated A4 sign saying "GLIDER PILOT". If you land out away from where you took off, it will help if you can show you have a legitimate reason for hitchhiking.

Survival bag: of the large thick bin-liner style. Sit on it if the ground is damp. Put yourself in it in an emergency. Put your glider bag in it if there's a sudden shower.

Miniature bottle of whisky or similar: when you've just landed far away on a grouse moor and the game keeper comes to tell you off, a smile and a little present can work wonders, plus you might get a lift from them.

Little packet of sweets: when you've just landed in a park and some kids come over and say "where have you come from?" a smile and a little present can work wonders, plus you might get a lift from one of their mums or dads.

BHPA card: carry this with your glider at all times. More on why in the section on coaches.

Most active sports have a well-defined, even obvious set of levels of progression. At one extreme are sport martial arts like Tae Kwon Do, where there's a very tightly prescribed range of techniques to be learned and demonstrated in a particular order at every level, and a rigidly-defined coloured belt to denote progression through the syllabus. Every time you go out of the house to "do" TKD, there's someone there who will take you through what you need to learn and how to do it.

Paragliding is very much the opposite. Once you're CP rated, you're on your own. Your continuation training is entirely in your own hands, and you have to be motivated and a self-starter to make progress at all. There are a couple more "belts" – Pilot and Advanced Pilot ratings – but if the BHPA will forgive me, these are to an extent box-ticking exercises designed to ensure you're insurable for cross country flying and high level competitions, respectively. The syllabuses are not (and are not intended to be) a training plan to improve your skills, they're a shopping list to fill to get the badge.

Nobody is going to come and rouse you from your bed, point out the window and say "perfect conditions today, we're going to be practicing your top landings!"

The resources to learn from are out there – this book is one of them – but you have to seek them out for yourself. A later section gives some personal recommendations for useful resources to save you some time.

The first question you need to ask yourself, however, is what you want to get out of the sport, as this will inform your training regime. Also, as you progress, your answer may change.

> *Personal Lesson: When I started paragliding, my intention was that it would be a bit like windsurfing or surfing – I'd turn up, fly around a bit, land by my car, and go home. Furthermore I decided to manage the risk of flying by placing a limit on my activities – I'd log 100 hours, then go and learn something else. The XC bug has since bitten me hard, so my plans have changed...*

Some people may be quite happy on a relatively safe, low rated wing, surfing up and down a ridge or dune, landing by their car and going to the pub. This is a perfectly valid choice, but don't be fooled into thinking you don't need to practice much. You are still flying, and it's still a serious undertaking, and good preparation combined with staying current will make it safer and more enjoyable for you, and for the other people you share the air with.

One thing you probably will see, if your local site has the potential, is people turning up, taking off, and disappearing up into the sky and over the back of the ridge and away. You may later hear that they landed after several hours, dozens of miles away. It may occur to you to wonder how this is possible, and whether you could do the same. The answer is yes, and there are things you can start doing *right now* to prepare yourself for your first cross country flights.

Another thing you'll probably see at some point is someone turning up with something that looks like a paraglider but smaller, possibly much, much smaller, and launching it in a wind speed where you'd not even think about taking your glider out of the bag. Speedwings – paraglider-like wings with an area of less than 20m² – are becoming more and more popular, and their small size, responsiveness and ability to fly while you're stuck on the deck can make them look easy and tempting. Do not be fooled, however – they are definitely not for novices. They fly fast, sink fast, react fast, and when things go wrong, they go wrong fast. They're a lot of fun, too – but get plenty of paragliding experience under your belt before you clip into one, and if at all possible, get some instruction.

You may see videos on the internet, and if you're lucky you may see in person, people throwing their gliders into manoeuvres with names like SAT, infinity tumble, helico and misty flip. Acro flying is where paragliding becomes a true extreme sport, and is strictly for experts only. Even then, acro pilots will usually train and perform over water, with a safety boat in attendance, and sometimes fly with not one but two reserve parachutes. You too can do acro – there are plenty of places in Europe and elsewhere that offer training, but as with speedwings, get plenty of paragliding experience under your belt first.

Ultimately, you may get a bit competitive, and want to start objectively comparing how well you're flying against your peer group, locally and nationally. There are two ways to do this.

All year long, various online leagues allow you to upload your qualifying flights and compare your performance against other pilots, in your local area and across the country. There is no structure to this competition beyond a certain agreed set of rules – you can fly wherever and whenever you like.

Alternatively, you can enter a specific competition, where pilots will gather in a particular region to fly defined tasks round turnpoints to an agreed goal.

There's some brief discussion of how to prepare and enter these competitions in a later section.

SIV stands for "Simulation d'Incident en Vol", or in English, simulation of incidents in flight.

On an SIV course, you will put your glider through a series of manoeuvres designed to demonstrate to you the limits of its performance (and yours…). You'll fly as fast and as slow as your glider will go, and learn to recognise how it behaves at these extremes. You'll turn 90, 180 and 360 degrees as fast as it's possible to do on your wing.

You'll be intensively briefed and coached as you perform descent techniques including big ears, really BIG big ears, B-line stalling and spiral dives.

You'll deliberately cause your glider to collapse and otherwise fail in various ways, and learn how to deal with what follows, up to and including deliberately spinning and stalling then recovering the wing.

And you may be taken through the most basic manoeuvre in acro flying, the wingover. Wingovers look easy, but big, smooth, symmetrical wingovers are deceptively difficult to pull off and are also a good deal more dangerous than they look if you get them wrong, as you can see if you search Youtube for the word "wingover".

The ideal SIV venue is a mountain several thousand feet high, with good, convenient transport from the bottom to the top, positioned right next to a lake or the sea so all the training can be done safely over water. There are no such places in the UK, so if you want to do an SIV course it will mean going abroad. Most UK residents go to France, Switzerland or Turkey for their courses.

The BHPA offer guidance on how to choose an SIV course, but they do not certify courses. The best way to choose a course is by personal recommendation from a pilot you know.

You may wonder whether you're ready for an SIV course, or whether you should wait until you're more skilled. Here's my take on that:

Do it, do it now, and plan on doing it again later.

Your first SIV will be a nerve racking experience. You will learn more than you might realise at the time, and mainly what you will learn is not to over-react. You will learn that, other things being equal, a low-end glider (EN A or low-end EN B) wants to fly, and that if you get out of the way and let it, it will usually do just that. This is not something you can learn from a book, however – you have to experience it personally. Don't assume because it's written here that your glider is bomb-proof – nothing is. The only way to find out just how much you can trust your wing is to take it on a course and, under supervision, deliberately make it stop flying normally, then see how, and how quickly, it recovers.

It should boost your confidence in your wing immensely, and that alone should improve your flying. You will most likely also experience just how fast things can happen, which should give you a healthy respect for the limits of your abilities. In summary, you should do an SIV as soon as possible.

Even with the best instructor in the world, some of what happens on your first SIV will be wasted on you. Don't worry about this. When your flying has improved to the point that you need a new wing, get that new wing and do SIV again.

You will learn more, and appreciate what you're learning more.

Personal lesson: some time after doing SIV, I was flying a new site. I'd had a good day, and done at least a dozen good top landings near the lip of the hill. At the end of the day I lazily decided to top land further back, closer to the car park. As I came in on final approach, I had a frontal collapse one onlooker described as "dramatic".

Had it happened to me before I'd done SIV, I'd have probably done one of two things: either immediately panicked, yanked the brakes hard in a misguided effort "to reinflate the wing" and stalled to a crippling or fatal landing; or frozen, and when the glider recovered and delivered me to earth I'd have packed it up and sold it.

As it was, I looked up and thought "oh yeah, seen one of those before, bugger", didn't over-react, but put my hands up with confidence that the wing would recover, ready to damp the surge when it did or take other action if it didn't. I've thanked the SIV instructor personally for making that possible.

YOUR LOCAL CLUB

You've got signed off as CP, you've bought a wing and a harness and you've prepared them for flight. You've packed your bag with some or all of the other kit recommended. What now?

Step one should be to join your local club, if you've not already. It's your local club that manage access to flyable hills in your area. They do the delicate negotiating with landowners that allows flying to happen. Set next to the cost of a wing and harness, or even just a decent helmet, club membership is pretty reasonable. Joining will also put you in touch with the people best placed to give you the advice and coaching you're going to need over the next weeks and years.

They'll also be responsible for setting up social and educational events related to flying, at which you can meet the other people who fly in your area, introduce yourself, and talk about flying. This is very important. Your friends and relatives will be absolutely enthralled to hear about your flying exploits... the first few times. Soon enough, when you start to talk about orographic cloud or having needed to use full bar to stay forward, they'll start to glaze over. People who know what you're talking about, and more importantly care, are a valuable resource. Cultivate them.

CLUB COACHES

There will be, in your local club, a number of pilots who've attended a BHPA course to qualify them as club coaches. You should be able to get a list of their contact details from the club. They are a valuable source of information, hints, tips and advice. Get to know one or more of them.

Club coaches are **not instructors**. It takes a great deal of training, time, effort and expense to become a paragliding instructor, and there are significant written exams that you need to pass.

To become a club coach, you need Club Pilot plus ten hours flying experience. That's not a typo – as soon as you can dump the red ribbon, you've done enough to apply to be a coach. There is no exam – you just attend the two day course and then need to be signed off as suitable by your club's senior coach or chairman.

Most coaches, of course, will have more experience than this – some of them much, much more. That said, it can be helpful to be coached by someone who has relatively fresh memories of being new to the game, so low-airtime coaches are valuable.

Because coaches are not instructors, they are neither trained nor insured to deal with you until after you've got your CP rating. If you're an enthusiastic trainee with just a couple of tasks left to get signed off, and you've taken your wing to the local landing zone for a bit of ground handling practice, the only advice a coach is in a position to give you is "don't". They may be tempted to offer more, but they are putting both you and themselves at risk by doing so.

Don't put them in that position.

Until you've got your CP rating, only take your glider out under the supervision of an instructor. **This means ground handling too**.

For this reason, carry your BHPA card with you whenever you go flying. If you can show that you're CP rated, club coaches will generally be more than happy to help you however they can.

For reasons of courtesy and safety, if a club coach who has been helping you is in the process of preparing to fly, do not go over and ask them questions. We each have our own rituals and routines for preparing for flight, and it is important that these routines are not interrupted in case something vital is missed. If a coach is walking round the hill with their helmet off, by all means approach them, but if they're picking their harness up, ask someone else or save the question for later.

It may seem a bit presumptuous ringing a stranger out of the blue and asking them for advice, but remember they've volunteered for the role of coach.

A coach's role is not to teach you, more to guide the process of you teaching yourself. They will encourage you to start thinking like a pilot, taking in the information you need to make the right decisions and to take responsibility for those decisions.

YOUR HOME SITE

Find your local club's site guide, and read it, ideally in conjunction with a 1:25,000 OS map of the area (assuming you can read a map...). Identify the site that will become your "home" hill, the place where you will have most of your most important early flying experiences.

The ideal "home" hill for the beginner might look like this:

- Reasonably close to, and ideally visible from, your home or place of work
- Top driveable, or not too long or strenuous a walk

- A long, soarable ridge that doesn't generate strong, turbulent thermals, but where some thermal lift can be found on the right days
- Faces towards the prevailing wind direction, i.e. "works" reasonably frequently
- Has a large, flat, unobstructed, well-drained, grassy landing field within sight and easy glide of the take off point
- Has a handy landmark which indicates when you're low and should either slope land or head for the landing field
- Has plenty of space to top-land
- Has a smooth, not too steep slope on which to side-land
- Is smooth and grassy without rabbit holes, rocks, heather, thornbushes, barbed wire fences etc.
- Has no scary obstacles immediately downwind such as spine back ridges, wind turbines or conifer forests
- Isn't in or close to restricted airspace or private land
- Doesn't have any areas of nasty turbulence
- Is reasonably regularly flown by experienced pilots from whom you can pick up tips
- Isn't excessively crowded

If you know of or find a site that fits all those criteria, probably best keep it to yourself or it will rapidly be very crowded indeed.

Now you've found your site, read the site guide for it again. And again. Look at any photos you can find of it. Look at it on the map, and on Google Earth. Start to watch the weather reports (see later), paying particular attention to how they will affect your site specifically.

Eventually you can visit your home site for the first time as an independent, CP rated pilot.

Before you go, check your gear bag one more time. Attach your glider to the harness and carefully concertina pack it. Make sure everything you need is in your bag, and that your bag and boots are in the car. You don't want to arrive fully equipped except for your helmet...

FIRST HOME SITE VISIT

This is your first time out in the world as an independent pilot. For the first time, nobody is going to tell you authoritatively that it's OK to launch – the decision is yours alone. You ought to be a bit daunted by the prospect.

Equally, though, it shouldn't daunt you too much – you **can** do this. Your instructor would not have signed you off if they didn't think you could. So have confidence in yourself, tempered with caution your first few times out.

It may occur to you on your first visit that it would be easier to leave your glider in the car and simply walk up and check out the site. Don't do this.

On the one hand, if you stick with this paragliding lark, you're going to need to get used to making this walk fully loaded. You might as well start getting used to it right now.

On the other hand, imagine how frustrating it will be if you walk for ten or thirty minutes or more to the top of the hill to find perfect conditions, and then have to walk back to the car to get your glider. Imagine how much more frustrating it will be when you arrive back at the top to find the wind has dropped or it's started raining, and you could have at least flown down if you'd only brought it up the first time.

FIRST SETUP

It's your home hill, and your first visit. You've slogged up to takeoff with your wing. Is there anyone else there?

If not, dump your bag and have a look around. Try to relate what you can see to what you've read in the site guide. Find the landmarks – walls, fences, gullies – that will usually feature in site descriptions. Picture the way the air will flow over the hill and generate lift. Look at where you can top land, or slope land. Try to picture where the lift band will be, and where any turbulent spots might develop. In short, start to develop your skills of thinking like a pilot.

If there is someone there on the ground, and they're not on the point of launching, go talk to them. Ask if they're a member of the local club. Ask their opinion of the conditions. Tell them, upfront, that it's your first time on the site. They will likely be very forthcoming with information on stuff you need to know.

If other, experienced pilots are staying on the ground – leave your glider in the bag. One day, you will be good enough to be wind dummy. Today is not that day.

If there's someone else already flying, don't assume it's OK for you to fly. The person you can see might be the local nutter, who'll launch into anything regardless of whether it's

60

advisable using a wing they got on eBay. It might be a complete skygod whose instinctive control over the pitch and pressure of their high-performance wing makes a horrible, shearing mess of turbulent air look smooth and inviting. Or they might be muttering "ohshitohshitohshitohshit" and wishing they were you, safely on the ground. The first time you turn up, there's simply no way to tell.

One helpful indicator, though, is how much and how often they're turning. If you can see someone flying, but they're just sitting there pointing into wind with their hands up and their legs locked out straight to the front, not moving very much, they're probably not having a particularly fun time. Stay and watch, and when they land – which will probably be before very long – make sure they're OK and ask them how they got on.

Assuming everything's looking good, it's time to prepare to fly.

I've found it helps to develop a specific routine for preparation, to do the same things in the same order every time. Start developing the right habits from day one.

Open your bag and take out your gloves, helmet, clothing and instruments. Leave the glider packed for the moment.

Now is the time to do any diddling with electronics that you need to do. GPSs generally need a few minutes to establish their position, so switch yours on as soon as you take it out of the bag. If you have a radio, switch it on and do a radio check by simply keying the mike and saying "Radio check, radio check". If there's anyone else on channel and your radio is working, you should get back a "Loud and clear", to which you should respond "Thanks.".

If you ever need to do anything complex with your GPS – setting waypoints or routes, etc. – the time to do is now, while the glider is in the bag.

If you carry a mobile phone (and you should), switch it to silent.

> *Personal Lesson: My aforementioned very-soon-after-CP three hour flight was, for the last two and a half hours, punctuated at sixty second intervals by an insistent "beep" from my mobile, letting me know that someone had rung and left me a message. I could have landed and sorted it out. I should have switched it to silent before I took off.*

Once you're satisfied that your instruments are ready to fly, fasten one side of your cockpit to one of the carabiners.

Put on whatever clothes you're going to wear, get your gloves on (helmet too if you like) and then *and only then* start preparing the wing for flight. I'm going to recommend at this point that you don't open the wing out fully. I'm further going to assume that in preparation for your first flight, you've neatly concertina packed it. If this is the case, open out just a few cells in the centre of the leading edge, leaving the trailing edge gathered and the tips closed.

Once the wing is ready to go, check over your harness. If it's an airbag type, fluff the bag to get some air in it. In particular, ensure that the reserve handle is in place and attached, and that the pins are properly located. Gently pull the handle to separate the Velcro that holds it in place, then reattach it. If you don't know how to do this, ask someone to show you. The reason for doing this is that Velcro, if compressed for an extended period of time, can sometime lock quite tightly closed. "Exercise" your Velcro every now and then to make sure that, if you ever have to pull that handle, it will come clear easily.

Develop the habit of always checking the security of the reserve handle before you put on the harness.

Personal Lesson: more than once I've seen people top land sketchily, and take an amusing and entirely

Set your drinking system up so that the tube will be accessible but not obtrusive when you're flying.

Put your helmet on if it's not on already, step through your stirrup with one leg, hoist the harness onto your shoulders, and strap in.

At this point, you might want to take a couple of steps towards your wing to make sure the lines are fully slack and you're not going to inadvertently semi-launch while you're strapping in.

When you strap in, get into the habit of always doing so in the same order, and always start with your legs. I always start with the left, partly because of the setup of the Safe-T-bar style harness I use. Make sure you fasten all your harness straps **before** you start securing your cockpit.

Personal Lesson: Shortly after buying a cockpit, I did a launch with just my leg straps fastened. I'd done the leg straps first, which was good, but then secured the cockpit, and because I now had something strapped across my chest, I forgot the actual harness chest strap. Fastening the chest strap in flight is harder than you think, and in the event of a big collapse an open chest strap could lead to a very rapid cascade of serious problems. Always fasten all your harness straps before securing your cockpit.

Securing your cockpit should be a familiar sequence, because you should have practiced threading and fastening the straps with your harness hung up at home. Preparation in advance will save you messing about when you have more important things on which to focus.

This being the UK, you are most likely going to attempt a reverse launch, and once again it's time, if you haven't already, to start developing a habit of always turning the same way. This way, you'll develop the habit of always turning BACK the same way, and you'll be less likely to suffer the indignity and potential danger of a launch with twisted risers.

There is a school of thought that says you should be equally capable of reverse launching in either direction, in case you need to do so after a quick slope landing, or in a tight spot or on a cambered slope. Being able to reverse launch in either direction is indeed a valuable skill, and one you can focus on much later. For now and the immediate future, though, get that habit of always turning the same way embedded deep in your muscle memory from day one. It should eventually become the case that if you look down and the "wrong" riser set is on top, you immediately know there's something up.

It's a good tip, once you've set up and got yourself ready, to just sit down and take a few moments. Watch the clouds, if there are any. Watch the grass. See what the wind is doing. Is it getting stronger, weaker, gusting, getting smoother? What's upwind? Are there any birds or other gliders about getting lifted? You're fully prepared to inflate your wing, but there's no hurry – take in your environment, and start to think like a pilot.

Setup order:

1. Electronics out, switched on and checked.
2. Phone to silent and stowed somewhere reachable.
3. Cockpit attached to one carabiner.
4. Gloves on. Helmet too if it's cold.
5. All loose gear (compression straps, jacket, rucksack/stuffsack) secured in harness with zips fully closed.
6. Drinking system tube secured in a reachable position with valve locked shut.
7. Glider unpacked partially.
8. Harness checked – speed system attached and stowed
9. Reserve handle checked and Velcro exercised
10. Helmet on if not already.
11. Strap in fully.
12. Fix cockpit
13. Sit down and make ready.

GROUND HANDLING, WING WALKING AND REVERSE LAUNCHING

You are now ready to begin ground handling. Specifically, you should never start ground handling until you've done all of the above.

I'll concede that if you're just doing a practice session on your local soccer pitch, you don't actually need to switch on your GPS or necessarily sort your drinking system. But that aside, even your ground handling practice sessions should follow the routine and pattern of a real flying day. The idea is to get your routine for checking everything ingrained as a habit, so that eventually it will start to happen more smoothly.

That said, never rely on habit entirely. The BHPA recommends a pre-launch mnemonic: "Will Geordie etc.?" The idea is that each of the letters will jog your memory for something you should have checked. Never stop going through that checklist before you inflate your wing.

Personal lesson: I was looking to trade up from the EN A wing I'd been flying for six years. I'd got a couple of wings from a dealer for demo purposes, and had just launched for the second time on one of them. Conditions were perfect, light but soarable wind at my extremely familiar home site. The only new factor in my day was the wing. I decided to test its performance, and pushed half speed bar. There was, I thought, a slight increase in wind noise, but it didn't seem like much. Speed bar action was smooth and easy – very nice. I pushed full bar. Still nice and easy, almost effortless, but the wing didn't seem to be going as fast as I'd expect. Then I noticed that only one of the brummel hooks was connected. I didn't actually have any bar on at all. My preflight check of "connections" had in fact only checked the carabiners. Check your brummel hooks. If you like, tape them together or if you never disconnect your wing and harness, consider using a vice or pliers to close them slightly and make separating them more difficult.

It is impossible to overstate the importance of ground handling practice.

When you first start, it will be hard work, as you'll be fighting the wing and doing more moving about than is really necessary. Your inputs will likely be large, late and possibly wrong. Don't be discouraged. There is no shortcut, but with practice you will improve to the point that you can use the wing to help you.

An important tip is to watch other pilots ground handle. Whether you realise it or not, you will, if you pay attention, subconsciously pick up techniques from them. For this reason, it's probably best if you only watch the ones who look like they're good at it...

There are many schools of thought on ground handling techniques, and many methods of launching. You can buy whole DVDs on this subject alone. Ultimately, however, once beyond the absolute basics this is something else you have to teach yourself. What follows is simply my preferred technique for reverse launches in UK conditions, based on what I was taught by instructors, what I found on internet forums, and what I found worked for me. Try it out, but don't forget to experiment with it and work out what works for you.

In my experience, there are two distinct phases of ground handling – facing the wing with it on or near the ground, and standing on the ground with the wing flying comfortably overhead.

WING ON THE GROUND – BRAKE HANDLES

The first priority while the wing is on the ground is to make sure you get the correct brake in the correct hand without any knots or twists around the risers. Techniques that involve taking off with the brakes in the wrong hands and letting go to swap just after launch are unnecessary and probably dangerous.

Start at the carabiner on one side, and follow the **rear riser** away from it. Sort out any twists, and you should find the brake handle sitting facing up at you waiting for you to get hold of it. Repeat on the other side. Do this **every time** you launch or ground handle. Even a slight twist in the brake riser, with the line threaded through a gap, can lead to the line sawing into the riser as you pull it or a jam at the crucial moment when you most need full control.

69

While ground handling, I prefer to thread my whole hand through the brake handle to avoid any possibility of dropping the brakes, something which when you're practicing is quite likely.

There are those who argue that actually flying like this is dangerous, as in the event of a bad collapse with twists you may find you can't get your hand out and can't get to the reserve, which could be (indeed, has been) fatal. My view is that if you subscribe to this theory, you can very easily remove your hands from the handles immediately after launch. While you're on the ground, it's better to be "hands through".

WING ON THE GROUND – RISERS

The primary aim here is to have full authority over the wing, avoid being dragged, and get the wing from the ground to above your head as smoothly as possible. The most versatile and reliable technique I've found is "A's and C's", sometimes referred to as the "Mitsos" method after one of the claimed developers of the technique.

This technique takes some practice, but one advantage is that it very quickly gives very strong authority over the wing with little tendency to drag.

With hands through the brakes, facing the wing and with the lines slack, arrange both sets of risers so that the As are on top with no twists.

Three things should hit you about the pictures above. If you're me, the one on the left looks OK, and the one on the right looks wrong. If after a top or side landing I face the wing and my risers look like they do on the left, I know I'm ready to go. If they look like they do on the right, I know I have to do a little pirouette before I can take off with my normal turn direction. Note: I couldn't describe to you how the risers look when they're "right" without thinking hard about it. But I've seen it so often that it's now habituated.

Obviously if you're not me, the one on the right might be perfectly OK and the one on the left is the "wrong" one. That is, of course, fine. The point is to ground handle so much that you know at a glance without thinking about it whether you can take off with your normal turn direction or not.

The other two things that should strike you about the photos are "Oi, he's wearing trainers!" and "He's got no gloves on!". Behind-the-scenes secret – this photo was taken in my garden and the glider was in its stuff sack. I *never* take it out without my gloves on.

With your dominant hand, palm up, grasp both/all the A risers at the maillons. You may need to turn your hips to even them up. It is **extremely important** that they are perfectly even in your hands, so take a few moments to make sure they are.

Now with the other hand, palm DOWN, reach down and through the dangling risers and grasp both sets of C risers, again as evenly as possible at the maillons.

The principle at this point is that pulling the A risers will make the wing go, and a strong pull on the Cs will make it stop. The C risers give more authority than the Ds or brake because their travel is shorter, and when pulled they spill wind from the trailing edge, reducing the effective area of the glider.

If you've laid out the glider as suggested on page 64, you can now inflate it and get it to unfold itself. Keeping close hold of the C risers, step back to put some tension in the As. If there's any wind at all, a little gentle pulling on the A risers should see the wing begin to inflate and unfold from its neat concertina pack. If it's happening too fast, or you're at all nervous or unsure what to do, step forward slightly and pull the C risers hard. You should find that this will drop the wing very quickly to the ground.

Once the wing is unfolded, practice inflating and deflating it by alternating pulls on the As and Cs. You should at this point inspect the lines to ensure you don't have any tangles. If you do, pull the Cs hard, walk towards one wingtip, and sort them out before proceeding.

If your wall is uneven, step towards the high side. If when you pull the As one side has a tendency to come up quicker, check that you have the risers evenly lined up in your hand.

This might seem an obvious point, but set up your wing according to the direction of the wind, not the slope. Taking off when the wind is *slightly* off the slope is perfectly possible. Doing so by stubbornly running directly down the hill as if the wind is blowing straight up the hill is not.

It is possible, using the As and Cs technique, to steer the wing in the air, even though you have all the A risers in one hand. Bear in mind that tension on the As will cause the wing to accelerate. Therefore, if you want the wing to fly to the RIGHT, you want to make the left side of the wing (as you look at it) fly faster, you need to put more tension on the left A lines (as you look at them), by pulling ALL the A lines to the RIGHT. Pull the As to the side you want the wing to fly.

Conversely, keep in mind that tension on the C lines will cause the wing to brake. If you want to slow down the left side of the wing, you need to tension the Cs on the left side, by pulling ALL the C lines to the right.

You will therefore usually be pulling the As and Cs in opposite directions to steer.

WING WALKING

If you have the wing balanced perfectly in front of you, you can (in anything other than very light or very strong winds) control how high off the ground the wing flies. If you want it higher up, gently release the tension on the C lines. If you want it lower down, pull the C lines harder.

This is an excellent technique for wing-walking, the incredibly useful skill of setting up low down the hill and having the wing gently tow you up the slope to the point where you wish to take off. Simultaneously balancing the pressure in the wing, steering it, and walking up the hill will save you a good deal of energy once you have mastered it, and is particularly invaluable on light wind days when you find yourself low down the slope having lost lift.

A useful exercise is to set up low down, then practice wing walking up the hill. At first, try to just balance the As and Cs to allow you to walk up the hill in a straight line. At first you will need to do this in hops. Keep practicing until you can keep the wing in the air a couple of metres off the ground as you walk towards it.

Then accelerate one side by pulling the As away from it, and follow the wing as it heads in the relevant direction. Bring the wing back to straight flight, still walking up the hill, then accelerate the other side similarly.

You will quickly learn that, in gentle winds, with the long lines and large surface area of a paraglider, it is relatively slow to react to your inputs. You therefore need to learn to anticipate what you want to do, and start making the correct inputs a second or two ahead of time. When you make adjustments, do so slowly and smoothly. If you drop a lot of tension out of the C lines quickly, the wing will surge and you may have problems.

There are plenty of videos on the internet and DVDs that purport to teach you this and other methods of launching.

Ultimately, however, there is no substitute for practice, and lots of it.

Personal lesson: if there's enough wind to inflate your glider, but not enough wind to soar, there's enough to practice ground handling. Don't sit around chatting waiting for the wind to pick up – practice your kiting.

Eventually, you will want to get the wing above your head and flying. It is most important that before you do this you make sure that the airspace around you is clear. You may well have done your "Will Geordie..." checks when you first strapped in, but how long ago was that? Ten minutes? Two minutes? Thirty seconds? Even a few seconds is long enough for someone to turn up apparently out of nowhere and try to top land next to you or indeed on top of you. EVERY time you consider lifting your wing off the deck, be paranoid about what's above and around and especially behind you.

Gradually release the tension on the C risers and let the wing fly up. When it's approaching zenith, you need to do a move that, to say the least, will take some practice to get right. You've probably done it, or something close to it, quite a few times in training, and got it right perhaps more by luck than judgement. I refer to doing ALL of the following:

- Dropping the C risers altogether
- Almost immediately after that, letting go of the A risers
- EITHER stepping smartly towards the wing to avoid being dragged (in a strong wind) OR stepping slightly AWAY from the wing and leaning down to keep it loaded (in a light wind)
- Pirouetting under the wing to face the direction of takeoff
- Applying some gentle brake to prevent the wing from overflying you but not so much that you get lifted or stall the wing and get dragged
- Keeping the wing facing directly into wind and flying

The action I'm referring to is probably the single most complex physical skill in paragliding that most people ever need, and it all has to happen in the space of less than a second, so don't beat yourself up if you don't get it right straight away. Keep practicing.

INVOLUNTARY TAKE OFFS

You may find, particularly if you've misjudged the wind and it's slightly stronger than you thought, that you perform an involuntary and perhaps vertical takeoff before you're fully ready.

If you do DON'T PANIC – in fact, relax and don't do anything for a second or two. If you've prepared for your flight correctly – right site, right wing, no tangles, brakes in the correct hands – the wing will fly. In particular DON'T pull the brakes, don't wriggle about trying to get into your seat, don't fiddle with your instruments or harness or radio. If you're in the air and didn't mean to be – relax. Fly straight away from the hill if possible. At this point, altitude is your friend – get as much air under you as you can for those first seconds. Check around to make sure you're not in anyone's way, and once you've taken a few seconds to settle yourself, make sure you're flying a safe course.

You may, if you've really misjudged things, find yourself going backwards. At this point, you'll need to use the speed bar. Get your hands up, and push the bar as far as you need to get forward speed. Steer with weightshift only.

Unless you have seriously, wildly misjudged the wind, you should find it possible to get to the landing field. Assuming this to be the case, head there immediately. Don't consider slope landing or top landing if it's windy enough to snatch

77

you off the hill – get to the landing field, land, and pack up. Think about what caused you to take off in such unsuitable conditions, and resolve not to do it again. There are some tips on high wind landings later.

WING IN THE AIR – BRAKES

The skill I was most envious of early in my paragliding career was the ability some pilots had to stand calmly at takeoff with the wing poised motionless above their head while they scanned the horizon or chatted with their mates, never looking up, just holding it there apparently effortlessly. Furthermore, they were able, when they wanted, to just walk to any other spot on the hill, and the glider would seem to follow like an obedient puppy. This seemed to me to be a near-magical level of control over the brakes.

Now, a couple of hundred hours on, I can't pretend I have that magical level of control, but I do realise a couple of things.
First, standing on the hill and controlling the glider above your head is excellent practice for this "active flying" thing you hear about – the business of instinctively controlling the pitch of your glider when in the air to fly efficiently and avoid or deal with collapses.

Second, there's more to it than just the brakes. There's also a subtle level of weightshift control going on as well, but to the untrained eye it's almost invisible. Nevertheless, watch a competent pilot kiting the wing above their head – observe in particular the bend in their knees, the position of their hips, and the movement of their feet. They're not just standing there – they're in constant dynamic motion, to an extent they probably don't even realise, any more than you realise the constant tiny balance corrections you make when you walk along.

For now, assuming you've not suffered the indignity of an involuntary takeoff, take some time to practice keeping the wing above your head.

At first, and for quite some time, you'll feel the need to look up at what the wing is doing. Resist this urge. Everything you need to know about what the wing is doing is being communicated to you by the pressure through the risers and the brakes.

KITING – STANDING STILL

Your first target should be simply keeping the wing still above your head. You can practice this even in winds too light to soar, so if there's enough wind to get the wing up, practice practice practice.

The basic position is standing facing directly into the wind with the glider above your head and the brakes in your hands. You should be applying about equal pressure on both brakes, just the weight of your arms or so, to give you some feel for what is going on.

It's apparent that there are really only a few things that can happen. Either the wing will surge forward, drop back, or start moving to one side or the other. Possibly, in a light wind, it may lose lift and start to collapse.

If the glider starts to drop back behind you, the brakes will both pull. If that happens, let up and let the glider fly. Note that you only need to do so for a second or so, then get back to normal pressure. At first, your movements will be jerky, and so will be the glider's responses. As you practice, your inputs will become smoother, and smaller, to the point you'll be barely aware of making them.

As they say in Aikido – beginners make big circles, masters make small circles.

If the glider surges ahead both brakes will go light. In this case, dab the brakes. What does "dab the brakes" mean? Try a smooth, firm, fast movement downwards by about a foot, letting up smoothly immediately. Again – don't expect to get the pressure or the distance right the first time. Have faith that it will come with practice.

If the glider starts to turn to the left, the right brake will start to pull. Pull back, to get the glider flying straight again. The left brake will go light – let it up a little to let the left side accelerate.

Obviously the reverse applies just the same.

In a light wind, you may feel the upward pull on the harness go light. While this may be a blessed relief of the crushing pressure on your groin, it's a sign that the glider is losing lift and is in imminent danger of a collapse. If the upward pull on the harness lessens, lean forward and try to get your body weight onto your chest strap. This will keep the load on the wing and keep it inflated.

KITING – MOVING AROUND

Sooner or later you're going to want to move to a slightly different spot on the hill. Possibly someone has arrived and set up in front of you, or the wind direction has changed slightly. In any case, you don't want to bring the wing to the ground, gather up the lines and sling it over your shoulder and carry it – kiting it across the hill is much less effort, and of course looks a hell of a lot cooler.

Moving backwards is easy enough. Squeeze on slightly more brake and simultaneously step back. Be careful where you walk, and also note that if you turn to look over your shouler you're inevitably going to unbalance the pull on the risers. So maybe not so easy at first.

Moving forwards is even easier. Keeping some pressure on the brakes, lean strongly forwards, applying pressure to the chest strap with your sternum. Do not move forward by sitting back or down into the harness. You will be likely to lose your footing, and the control you have will be minimal at best. Bear in mind that if you lean forward too enthusiastically you may take off, so be careful and be ready.

It took me a good deal of time get a grip of making lateral movements, until I heard this simple tip – start your trip by taking a step the wrong way.

Suppose you want to go to the left. Take a strong, positive step to your RIGHT. At this point, you're now no longer centralised under the wing, and it will start to roll left. The idea is that, having initiated that roll, you keep the angle constant by immediately starting to walk along to the left under the wing, just keeping up with it. When you want to stop, speed up your walk a bit until you catch up with the glider, and centralise it back above your head. Job done.

Again, judging how far to one side to step, and how fast you have to walk to keep up with, and overtake and stop, the wing, and how much brake to apply, are things you can only learn by practicing. The precise strength and depth of inputs needed cannot be measured or prescribed – they're a muscle memory thing, and the more you practice, the better you will get.

The simple step of taking one positive movement in the wrong direction, though, should set you up at least with the wing going the right way.

FORWARD/ALPINE LAUNCHING

British pilots are notoriously poor at Alpine launching, for the simple reason that we get very few opportunities to practice, and in any case rarely have the need for the technique. The forward launch is used to launch in nil-wind conditions from large mountains when one is reasonably certain there are reliable thermals out front over the deep valley. This set of conditions is common in the Alps and other big mountain ranges.

A rare nil wind day in the UK, by contrast, is at most sites a recipe for a sled ride to the bottom of the hill. For this reason, in absolutely nil wind most pilots don't bother even to walk up, and if they do walk up they'll likely wait around on the off chance a thermal cycle blows through to give them enough breeze to reverse launch.

Your forward launch skills will therefore quite likely get rusty quickly. This section can't offer much to affect that near-inevitability other than to repeat, yet again, the "practice" recommendation.

If it really is a completely nil-wind day, you can practice forwards on a flat field. This is worth doing if you get the chance, just to remind yourself how to do them.

The only other thing I'll offer regarding forward launching is – if it's truly nil-wind, then take plenty of time to lay out your glider properly. In training, you likely did your required forward launches in something other than entirely nil-wind, and this may have made you feel that you need to get the wing laid out quickly and then get clipped in and launched quickly, before the breeze blows the glider about. If there's enough breeze to cause you this problem, there's enough breeze to do a walking or running reverse launch. Save the forwards for when there's really absolutely no wind at all.

If your training was like that, you may not realise just how hard and for how long you have to run for a truly nil-wind forward launch, especially on a relatively gentle slope. Lean forward strongly – really get your weight onto your chest strap, keep running hard, and don't relax when your feet come off the ground – keep them down and ready to run again if your glide angle isn't taking you clear of the hill quite yet.

Assuming there's no absolutely no wind, there's no hurry. Lay the wing out on its back somewhere with the minimum of line-snagging obstacles on the ground such as rocks or thorny plants. You may choose to lay it out in a V shape with the tips closer to the harness. This will make the centre cells inflate first. However you choose to set up, make it neat and tidy and symmetrical. Set up the harness close enough to the wing that the centre A lines aren't tight, but far enough that there's not a lot of slack.

Take time to sort through the lines. Starting with the D risers on one side, gently tease out the lines, removing any loops, knots or tangles. Take care to look for stray twigs, thistles etc. Once the D lines on one side are clear, move to the Cs, then the Bs, then finally the As. By doing them in this order, you don't disturb the lines you've already sorted. Repeat on the other side.

Realistically, if you need to forward launch in the UK, you're probably not going to stay up. So take the time to savour the environment as you prepare. Don't rush.

In forward launching, more so even than in other areas of flying, preparation really is everything. If you prepare properly, your forward launches will be smooth and quick and without incident. You will, if you get it right, wonder what all the fuss was about. If you do wonder, watch someone who has rushed or otherwise hasn't prepared properly try to do one. And when they fail, help them out.

Finally, if there's someone else on the hill who can watch you launch, this can be a big help. Agree with them in advance a simple convention: if everything's going OK – glider's come up straight, no tangles etc. – then they stay quiet. If you hear them shout anything at all, you will assume they mean "STOP", and abort the launch.

THE COBRA LAUNCH

The standard reverse launch all pilots are taught has a weakness obvious to anyone who has had dealings with traction kites on land or sea, and even more obvious to anyone who has suffered a dragging from a paraglider in a strong wind. Between the moment where your wing is sitting docile on the ground as a nice symmetrical wall and the moment where it arrives above your head, under control and about to carry you into the sky, it first passes directly through what kite flyers call the "power zone" – the position of maximum lateral pull.

When launching in a high wind you need to minimise the bad effects of this by a combination of quick, decisive launching, firm pressure on your C risers to spill wind as the wing rises, and moving smartly towards the wing to take the power out of it, followed by a rapid dab of the brakes to prevent it surging over you.

Or… you can try a cobra launch.

The principle of the cobra launch is that you set up the wing at an angle to the wind instead of square on, then using one A riser and the corresponding brake, you bring up the wing tip first at the edge of the wind "window". Instead of having it move vertically up in front of you, you kind of slide it up over your head from the side. The wing's full area is never exposed to the wind.

Done right, it's very impressive. At the start, the bulk of the wing is pinned to the ground, and the wingtip rears up and weaves into the air like a snake, hence the name. A skilled exponent of the cobra can get their glider into the air without taking a step, even in a strong wind. For this reason it's especially popular with tandem pilots, who are having to deal simultaneously with a wing much bigger than a normal glider, plus a usually fairly clueless passenger.

The description of the technique is intentionally vague, as it's very much not recommended for beginners. It's mentioned here for the sake of completeness, because you will hear about it. Suffice to say that if it's windy enough that you need to cobra launch, it's probably too windy for you to fly, for now.

When you get good enough or curious enough to try out the cobra, there are plenty of online resources that will give you a more detailed description.

Note that the cobra launch actually requires quite a strong wind to work at all – you can't practice it in a light breeze. For that reason, take great care if you decide to try to learn it.

STRONG WIND LAUNCHING – DRAGGED AND TUMBLED

When launching (or landing) in a strong wind, there's an obvious risk of a dragging. If you do get dragged, don't panic. Grab the nearest single line you can. Ideally, pull just one brake line, but in the heat of the moment don't be choosy. Haul it in hard. Keep hauling it until the glider is flagged out, and keep hold of it while you compose yourself. It is at this point you can be silently thankful that you were well prepared and wore your gloves.

There is always the possibility that in all the excitement you will step, fall or roll through one or all of your lines.

If this happens, STOP.

Get out of your harness.

Check very carefully to make sure your harness is the right way up, and that you've not got a riser twist.

CHECK YOUR RESERVE.

My own advice is – resist the urge to unclip the glider from the harness. You generated the twist while it was attached, you can probably fix it most easily and reliably while still attached. Most likely all you need to do is either tumble the harness forwards or backwards once, or pass the whole thing through the gap between two lines once. It can be a challenge working out what you need to do, especially if it's still really windy.

Twenty minutes spent sorting out a tumbled or tangled harness and wing is preferable to a launch with the problem still there.

Before you launch again, think about why you got dragged, and why on your next launch, you won't be. Did you move towards the wing fast enough to reduce its power? Did you take off during a gust, when you should have waited for a lull? Or is it just too strong, and is your best course of action a walk back down?

If you do take the walk back down, don't let it discourage you. Get out flying again as soon as possible, on a day with easier conditions. Congratulate yourself for your good judgement in taking the hint that the dragging gave you, and remember the lesson.

At last, here is a section offering some advice regarding actual flying.

Intentionally, however, there's not much. There are other, far more comprehensive resources that will teach you about how to fly your glider. What follows is just a very few hints and tips I've not seen mentioned much anywhere else, things which you might consider common sense, but which are easily forgotten in the rush of being airborne.

INSTRUMENT FIXATION

The first time you fly with an instrument that has a visual readout, it's fascinating. You first feel the change in lift through the seat of your pants, then a moment later your vario beeps, the analogue bar starts to fill, and the altimeter ticks up. Hey look, you're 100ft above take off! Look, you're 150ft above! 200ft!

Hey, look, you're about to have a mid-air collision with someone you should have seen ten seconds ago...

Unless you are flying under a very low airspace ceiling on a very good site on a very good day, you are unlikely to *need* to see your altimeter for a while. If you've followed my advice and bought an instrument that includes a GPS which records your position, you can look back at what altitude you reached later if you're really interested.

For now, switch the instrument on so it beeps when you go up, and don't look at it. Consider covering it with a bit of cloth or mounting it upside down to remove the temptation. Keep your head on a swivel and keep a lookout for other air traffic, all the time your wing is in the air (and that includes when your feet are on the ground).

Instrument fixation is by no means exclusive to complete beginners, and it's not just a safety issue.

Personal Lesson: I and several other pilots had gone over the back at my local hill. We were already 10km downwind in abundant gentle lift. At one particular point I was circling in zero lift, trying to find the next thermal. I started looking at the "last thermal" indicator on my GPS/vario. As I circled in silence, I was scrolling through the screens until I could see the readout showing how far I was from the last strong bit of lift I'd been in. I circled some more, working out exactly which direction it was in and wondering whether I should try to fly back upwind towards it. All the while my buddies, who were paying attention to the environment instead of staring into their laps, had found a cloud that was working and were climbing. I, on the other hand, although I was never at any risk of collision with anything, had drifted off track into a blue hole, too far from their cloud to make it into the lift, and glided to the ground well short of where they got to.

Don't fly into clouds. It's illegal and it's dangerous, especially if there are other paragliders or indeed any other aircraft at all about.

That said, if you fly for long enough, sooner or later you might find yourself in the white room.

Your first choice thing to do if you're in or approaching cloud should be big ears. You should know how to get them in and get them out and be completely comfortable with doing it. If you're not, practice in clear air. Get them in and hold them in.

If after a few seconds you're still going up, push on some speed bar. Whenever you apply speed bar, be ready at a second's notice to get off it fast if your wing does something unpleasant.

You should always do these things in the order big-ears, then speed bar.

If you were to apply speed bar first, there's a risk that yanking down the outer A lines on your accelerated wing will cause a bigger collapse than you'd like, whereas smoothly pushing bar when the ears are in actually stabilises the wing and returns its angle of attack to something close to what it's supposed to be.

To remember in which order to do them, simply insert your chosen stereotype for meanness (Scotsman, Yorkshireman, Peter from Accounts etc.) and think "be like them – go to the bar last".

If you've got the ears in and are on half bar and you're still going up, and the air is not too rough, give it some more bar.

90

Most EN A wings have pretty terrible glide performance when fully accelerated, and in this situation terrible glide is exactly what you want. Again, be ready to come off the bar in a hurry if anything untoward happens.

Research has shown that without navigational clues like the sun or landmarks, people will naturally walk in circles. They'll do this even if they're trying their best to walk straight, and they'll even believe strongly that they are in fact walking straight.

Inside a cloud there are no clues at all, and disorientation isn't just easy, it's inevitable. Add to that the fact that any tiny bias in your weight shift will make your glider fly in circles, and you'll be glad of your compass.

Clouds do not have sharp edges. Your journey from clear air to complete white-out is gradual. While you can still see, point your glider either directly away from any nearby terrain or other aircraft, or if you're clear of obstacles, at the closest edge of the cloud you're being sucked into. Aim for clear sky – that's where the sink is.

Once you're facing in the desired direction, take a look at your compass. This is a good time to fixate on an instrument, because once you're in the cloud there's nothing else to look at and, you hope, nothing to look out for. There's no need to try to take an accurate bearing – the nearest principal wind point (i.e. N, NE, E, SE etc.) is good enough.

Your mission, as you apply big ears and speed bar to try to get down out of your cloud, is to keep that compass, and hence your glider, pointing in that same direction, which if you've got it right should be the shortest route to sinking air.

You must of course steer by weightshifting, since with the ears in and bar on you can't use the brakes. Once you've got your ears in and speed on, focus on that compass and keep flying in a straight line.

There are alternative descent techniques, including the B-line stall and the spiral dive. These are techniques for experts.

The spiral dive in particular is not something you should attempt for the first time in an emergency over land. Just fly in a straight line away from the lift and out of the cloud. The faster you can do this, the better, but don't put full speed on if the air is rough or you're not comfortable.

Concentrate on maintaining your safe heading and getting away from the lifting air. This is the safest course for the low airtime pilot.

As a low airtime pilot, you'll spend most of your first few dozen hours in the UK ridge soaring.

Again, this book is not intended to teach you how to soar. Beyond the basics your instructor gives you to get to CP, it's something you have to teach yourself.

There are, however, a few tips relevant to the business of ridge soaring that it's worth passing on.

Check your airspace. When you're setting up to launch, your last check before you inflate and launch your wing should be the immediate airspace around you. That means in front, above, behind and to both sides. You are, most likely, standing where people like to top land. If you inflate your wing in the path of someone who's lining up for a landing, it could be very dangerous. Get a hold of those C risers and keep that wing firmly on the deck until you're sure the air is clear.

Conversely, once you're flying, have some consideration for people on the ground. Don't repeatedly "buzz" the takeoff area. Don't hang about, monopolising the lift band directly in front of the takeoff area – you're effectively stopping other people from taking off. Fly off down the ridge and give people space to get off. And if you want to top land, do so well away from anyone who is clearly setting up to take off. This obviously goes double if they're flying a red ribbon.

If lots of people are flying and it's getting hectic – land. There's always another day. As your skills improve you will become more comfortable with a crowded sky, at which point this advice will change to "don't land unless you absolutely have to", but discretion is always the better part of valour. If in doubt, land. You can always take off again.

If everyone else lands, ask yourself why. Then land, and ask them why. The answer might be "we stopped for a chat/cigarette/toilet break", in which case you can take off again and fly in the lovely empty sky. Equally, the answer might be "That, over there" and a finger pointed towards a horrible big black cloud you hadn't noticed. Early on, try not to be the first or the last person flying, and ask people why they made the decisions they did. Their answers will contribute to improving your decision making.

Then again, beware ground suck. If a bunch of guys you have got to know have landed for a ciggy and a natter, it can be enormously tempting to go and join them and be sociable. You can easily spend half the flyable hours of a day sitting on the side of the hill chatting. I'm not suggesting you should be anti-social, but have you come out to fly, or what? Assuming there's no reason to land – keep flying. Be assured – there will be plenty of days where you're able to sit on the hill chatting when the weather is preventing you from flying. If it's flyable – fly.

When you've got a few dozen hours, and if you're starting to think about going XC, you'll need to get comfortable flying when it's crowded. "Crowded" is a subjective term which can change depending on the pilot, the site and the conditions. On a good day, one side of my home hill can accommodate sixty gliders or more without a problem. The ridge is long, the lift band is large, and slope and top landing opportunities are vast. By contrast, with the wind from another direction and strong enough to require speed wings, four or five people diving about in the same narrow, turbulent lift band can feel worryingly hectic.

The fact is, though, that if conditions for XC flying are good, lots of people will be wanting to take advantage of them. The only way you can be one of those people is to be in the air. There are few things more frustrating than top landing and watching the people you were just flying with spiral up and over the back of the ridge, spreading out as they climb. Chances are if you launch at that point, you will not be able to connect with the bottom of the thermal they're in – which may be the last usable one of the day.

"You've got to be in it to win it". Don't put yourself at risk, obviously, but when you've got the experience, don't land just because there are a lot of gliders about.

One thing you will learn quickly is that if you do get into a thermal, what seemed like a dense crowd will very quickly thin out.

Personal Lesson: On the day of my personal best XC to date, something like sixty gliders were in the air at the same site. At one point, I briefly considered top landing to get out of the crowds. Ten minutes later, I was established in a climb with just one other glider anywhere near me, and the "crowd" had spread out over several dozen square miles and several thousand vertical feet. If I'd landed, I'd have missed that climb and one of the best flights of my life.

If you're ridge soaring and the lift starts to switch off, slope land **now**.

Don't think "I'll just do one more beat, it might pick up, and I'm bound to find some lift over that gully". It won't. You won't.

What you will do is find yourself several hundred feet further down the hill, below whatever lift band is left, with a hard walk back up carrying your glider over your shoulder and your vario beeping mockingly at you as go. I speak from bitter and repeated experience. This kind of thing is the very best motivation for learning to do really good slope landings.

Slope landings are another thing where watching someone who's good can really help your progress.

It can be quite intimidating flying at the side of the hill with the intention of hitting it under some sort of control. There is no substitute for practice in this regard.

When you come into land, get your legs down early. You'll likely see experienced pilots still in their pods three feet from the ground. You'll also see people stooshing in with their feet up, letting the airbags on their harness take the impact. This stresses the harness fabric and reduces its lifespan, plus it's dangerous. Don't be one of those people – land on your feet, and have them down sooner rather than later.

Every time you land, as you're approaching the ground, be thinking "PLF PLF PLF". Form the habit, even say it out loud if you like. That way if anything ever does go wrong, the right course of action will be on your mind already. Never be complacent – landing is one of the most dangerous phases of your flight, and if you've been flying for some hours you're likely to be tired. Stay alert until after you've landed.

Your landing is not over until you **and your wing** are safely down on the ground and the wing is secured out of the wind. Don't relax as soon as your feet are down – you haven't landed your aircraft yet.

Make your own decisions, and fly your own flight. If you're following someone, don't assume that because they make a particular spot that you will. If you have any doubts that you're going to make your chosen landing field, bail out early and go for another, closer one. A good landing in the wrong field is preferable to a crash in the right one.

> *Personal Lesson: Early on, I followed someone into my home site's landing field. He made it, and I thought I would too. I did – with just*

97

a few feet to spare over the wall and still needing to turn into wind. I turned, and found the wind direction in the LZ was different from that on the hill. I landed downwind, at speed. I didn't bail out early and land in the "wrong" field, as I should have done, and I didn't PLF. Two lessons, and two broken fingers. I was lucky.

In a nil wind landing, when you get your feet down, run and keep running. If you just stop, the wing may surge over your head and land nose down in front of you, or possibly just limply sink onto the top of your head. In either case, it's a tedious mess to sort out and it makes you look like an amateur. Keep running, flare and stall the wing down to a neat landing behind you. It will be much easier to pack from that position, plus it looks better.

HIGH WIND LANDINGS

High wind landings can be intense. In inversion conditions in the UK you'll sometimes find the lightest of breezes on the top of the hill, a layer of turbulence on the way down, and a strong wind in the landing field. Valley winds stronger than those on top are even more common in the really big mountains found abroad.

For this reason, don't fly past the upwind end of your landing field. Point into wind and check that you're penetrating. If you are, you can put in some gentle S-turns to bring you back over the field and land as normal.

If you are over the upwind end of the landing field and descending vertically, you're about to do a high wind landing. The most important thing to remember in this situation is that you must **not** flare. If you land in a high wind and apply the smooth, progressive symmetrical brake pressure you were taught in training, you'll be lifted up and backwards and dumped back on the ground several metres downwind, if you're lucky.

The priority in a high wind is to get the wing on the ground and depowered as quickly as possible while generating the minimum amount of lift or lateral pull to avoid a dragging. There are a number of techniques to do this. All of them require quick, decisive movements and a clear head. If you're descending vertically, don't panic, and take a moment to locate the controls you need so that you have them in your hands before you reach the ground. Your reaction when your feet touch down must be instant and authoritative, but not premature – the consequences of acting too early could be worse than the consequences of not doing anything at all.

The simplest technique is to stall the wing using the brakes. This is not at all like flaring. Take a wrap, or two, or three, of the brake lines, but keep your hands high and wait for your feet to touch down. When you're down, and not a second before, pull down both brakes as hard and as fast as you can, all the way down and hold them there. It should be a sharp motion, like you're trying to snap the brake lines. The wing should drop back behind you to the ground. IMMEDIATELY turn and run towards one wingtip, and if necessary grab a line near the tip or some of the glider itself to prevent it from refilling with air and powering up.

You can and should practice this technique when ground handling.

It is impossible to overstate the importance of timing when landing in a high wind. If you stall the wing from even a few feet off the ground you could easily be injured. Wait until you have positive contact with both feet on the ground, then and only then snap the lines down hard.

There are some other techniques you might see used in a high wind.

If the brakes don't give you enough authority (and the long brake travel and forgiving characteristics of beginners' wings may play a part here), consider getting hold of the D risers, or even the C and D risers while making your vertical approach. As with the stall landing, your pull must wait until your feet are firmly on the ground, must be swift and decisive, and should be followed by a sprint towards a wingtip.

Another technique I've seen and tried (but don't recommend) is to induce a frontal collapse by pulling down both the A risers on landing. Even more so than the stall, timing is everything. The theory is that the whole wing collapses very suddenly and drops almost vertically to the ground, generating no lift at all. My experience of this technique is that it's quite easy to get it slightly wrong, and when you do, especially on a lower rated wing, it can be nasty. What happens is the wing collapses, but doing its best to look after you, halfway to the ground it reinflates. It's now right in the power zone on a flat, windy field with you facing away from it. Not good. Practice this technique when ground handling and discover this difficulty for yourself, ideally in a lightish breeze.

A compromise technique which can work well is sharply to pull one A and one D riser. You get a 50%+ asymmetric collapse and the wing drops rapidly to the ground, with the pull on the D riser hopefully insuring you don't get an unplanned reinflation. You can end up with quite a tangled mess to sort out, but if it's windy enough to require this kind of landing, you'll be happy to be down in one piece.

Depending on the site, you may occasionally find yourself over the landing field going up and/or backwards. Don't panic.

If you're going up, pull big ears. Note that this will slow your glider down, so if you were going backwards before, you will be going backwards faster. Apply your speed bar as hard as you can. As ever with speed bar, be ready to come off it immediately if anything bad happens.

You are now in a relatively stable configuration, flying and descending as fast as you can. Steer gently with weightshift, and keep alert to the behaviour of the wing. Do not brake.

Under normal circumstances, you shouldn't pull *or release* big ears less than 100ft from the ground, in case doing so causes a collapse. Therefore, if you need big ears to get down, you need to hold them in all the way to the deck. Don't release them fifty feet up, because the disturbance to your wing, combined with the likely turbulence over the landing field in the high wind, could give you a problem.

Similarly, hold the speed bar on until you're as close to the ground as you can manage. Do try to come off your speed bar before you land, however, as landing on your feet is better than landing on your backside or your back.

If you land like this, release the big ears as you land and haul, hard and fast, on one riser and keep hauling. Bring the wing down by any means possible, and be braced for a possible dragging.

As previously stated, your preparation for your next flight begins as soon as your current flight ends. Take your time packing, even if you're tired and you've just had a tangle-inducing high wind landing. Time spent now will benefit you next time.

There is some debate as to whether one should detach the glider from the harness when packing. Many pilots will have been taught to do so and will perpetuate the practice without really thinking about it. It's a reasonable practice for schools because they need to mix and match wings and harnesses for different students, plus the exercise of connecting the wing to the harness is instructive.

However, if like most pilots you fly the same wing with the same harness every time, the value in detaching and reattaching is questionable.

On the one hand, proponents of separation say it's easier to pack the glider up smaller, easier to sort out tangles, not especially slower, and they appreciate the discipline of checking the connections every time.

On the other, those who prefer to remain attached say it's one less thing to check, one less thing to potentially get wrong, and that time spent reattaching is time wasted.

Whichever you prefer, question whether your preference is rational or just based on what you've always done. Experiment with the opposite, and make your own decision.

All that said, it's worth occasionally detaching and reattaching to remind yourself how to do it. No part of the assembly of your equipment should be unfamiliar to you.

A paraglider being ground handled is essentially a large bag, open on the top edge. Anything that finds its way in through your cell openings, e.g. thistles, grass, insects etc., tends to drop to the trailing edge and stay there. One pilot of my personal acquaintance took off and flew around for a while with a rock the size of a half-brick inside his wing. Another flew his powered paraglider around for three quarters of an hour with a live rabbit inside one of the cells (it survived the experience uninjured). My own wing seems to attract bees.

Anything left inside your wing when you pack could cause damage. In extreme cases, caterpillars trapped in a wing may eat their way out. More commonly, grit or sand in your wing is nastily abrasive, and you should make every effort to get as much sand out as you can whenever you pack.

Many gliders have what is charmingly called a "butt hole". This is an opening at the wingtip held closed with Velcro. By working your way down the wing shaking the contents from cell to cell, you can collect any internal detritus at one end, and drop it out of the butthole. Make sure you seal it back up properly.

There is a bewildering array of instruments available to the paragliding pilot. The following section gives some advice on how to choose one, how to use it in flight, and how to use it at home.

The important thing to realise is that, so far, nobody has invented the perfect paragliding instrument. If all you're doing is dune soaring, you don't need instruments. If you're just boating about at a ridge with no aspirations to go further, a simple audio vario is enough.

But if you have any aspirations to join the chase for more kilometres that is cross country flying or competition flying, you're going to need to carry two, or three, or more instruments.

If the perfect paragliding instrument existed, it would work as an audio vario, display statistics like how long you'd been in the air, your ground speed and glide ratio to a goal, would allow multiple waypoints and routes to be programmed in using a variety of coordinate formats, and give audio cues to alert the pilot that they were approaching, inside and/or leaving a specific area. It would be capable of displaying an up-to-date, uncluttered map of the nearby airspace at an easily-alterable scale, in colour, overlaid (if the pilot wanted) on a map of the terrain, with indicators where thermals might be generated. It would transmit the pilot's location in three dimensions via a cellular link to the internet to allow live tracking, and would record the pilot's tracklog in its memory at short intervals, with plenty of internal storage and a wireless connection to a PC for downloading flights to a free, intuitive, easy-to-use flights database manager. It would run for an extended period on just a couple of batteries, and would switch automatically to a second set of batteries when the first were exhausted, alerting the pilot to change them over when they get the chance. It would do all this with the minimal need for button pushing in flight, and would present information clearly on a screen readable in bright sunshine.

All of the features described above are available right now – just not all in one machine.

The right choices early on can save you money and time later on. As ever, preparation is everything.

CHOOSING AN INSTRUMENT

There are all sorts of instruments you might choose to use while paragliding. To simplify matters, I'll break them down into the following sub-categories:

- Altimeter/Varios
- Basic GPS/Varios
- Advanced/Competition GPS/Varios
- Dedicated Mapping GPSs
- PDAs/PNAs & open source software
- Phones with apps

ALTIMETER/VARIOS

Once the only instrument, other than a compass, that a paraglider would carry, the variometer is essentially a very accurate pressure meter, almost invariably connected to some sort of beeper to let you know what's going on without having to look at the instrument. For your first few soaring flights you don't need one. In fact, carrying one may actually be counter-productive – see the earlier section on instrument fixation. Nevertheless sooner or later you will want to start using one.

You can buy extremely light audio-only varios. This can typically be fixed to the helmet, and some veterans appreciate their simplicity and lack of fuss. They also function well as a backup if your main vario battery wears out in flight. Examples are the Renschler Solario and the Flytec Sonic.

More commonly a vario will have an "analogue" climb/sink rate readout, a digital indicator of same, and a readout of one or more of three altimeters. They will also automatically register when you take off and indicate how long you've been flying for.

At the time of writing in 2012, a new altimeter/vario can cost upwards of £200, with even the audio-only devices costing over £100. Examples include the Flytec 6005 and the Flymaster B1.

Personally, I believe these devices to be a waste of money. Unless you're on an extremely tight budget, you should really, even at this early stage, spring for the extra expense of a basic GPS/vario.

I say this because the additional features you get with such an instrument are worth far more in the long run than the approximately 50% extra you'll pay for one (at time of writing).

If you buy an instrument that's "just" a vario, sooner or later you'll buy a GPS as well, and will wish the two were integrated. You may even trade in the alti/vario for the next model up with integrated GPS. Don't make the mistake I did –

treat yourself to an instrument you can grow into and get the basic GPS model first.

BASIC GPS/VARIOS

These are usually laid out visually quite like their manufacturer's equivalent vario-only device, presumably so that they're familiar for people who are trading up, but do not be fooled. They are capable of much, much more.

The most important feature for the beginner is groundspeed indication. This is an invaluable safety aid, especially if you're quite high above the ground, which can make judging your groundspeed difficult or impossible.

If, when you are flying, your groundspeed when pointing into wind drops below a certain figure (say 10km/h or less), this is an indication that conditions are getting too strong and you should land, or at the very least get yourself into a safer position. If the compass rose on your instrument is pointing the opposite way to your actual compass, it means you're flying backwards and should get on the speed bar to get forward, and get away as soon as possible.

For my money the ground speed indication feature alone makes a basic GPS/vario worth the additional cost over a vario-only device for any new pilot.

A GPS/vario will, given a few minutes to think about it, set its own QFE, QNE and QNH altimeters. If you buy an alti/vario without GPS, you'll have to set two of these yourself every time you go flying. (Can you remember which?)

A GPS/vario will remember where you were the last time you were in lift, and will point you back towards that point.

When ridge soaring this isn't such an issue, but when you first start learning thermalling it's so useful it feels like cheating.

If you've got the space to do a reasonably slow 360 degree turn, a GPS vario will use the variation in your groundspeed around the circle to calculate the wind speed and direction. Obviously by the ridge you should be well aware of the direction and if you could launch the speed is just vaguely of interest as long as you're able to stay forward. However, this feature comes into its own when you eventually leave the hill and go XC to places where the weather might be quite different from where you launched.

Even basic GPS/varios will have basic competition-related functions like defining waypoints, setting up a route, and glide-to-goal calculation. Even if you never enter an organised competition, you can use these features to set yourself mini-tasks at your local site to give yourself something to aim for. More on this later.

Finally, and to me most persuasively, even most basic GPS/varios will record your flights in a huge amount of detail, allowing you to relive them, analyse them, and upload them, if they qualify, to online XC leagues and compete with your friends.

Your first few recorded tracklogs will likely consist of many repeated beats back and forth near the ridge. Analysis of these logs on something like Google Earth can show you the limits of what you're currently doing, and allow you to see how you can gradually expand those limits – flying further out from the ridge before you come back to top up with height, or fly further along and explore more of the lift band.

ADVANCED/COMPETITION GPS/VARIOS

These eye-wateringly expensive devices have all the features of their more basic equivalents plus the bells and whistles that top-level competition pilots want, including things like Macready Speed-To-Fly calculation, highly configurable displays, dedicated glide-to-goal screens and map/waypoint displays, and many more things I won't pretend to understand or care about. Suffice to say if you're the sort of person who's seriously considering spending seven to nine hundred pounds on a single flight instrument, you've probably forgotten more about flying than is contained in this book. Either that, or you have a great deal of spare money, in which case why not buy a copy of this book for each of your friends?

In seriousness, the upper end of the scale of GPS/varios really are optimised for people competing at the top level of the sport. You may, possibly, grow into one, but the likelihood is you'll never use most of what it's capable of and its additional features will be more of a distraction than a benefit.

DEDICATED MAPPING GPS

These are instruments which are not intended solely for paragliding, but are multifunction devices intended for walkers, sailors, pilots, geocachers, drivers and anyone else who needs to know where they are to some degree of accuracy on a moving map.

For the budding cross country pilot, the weakness of most basic GPS/varios is that they cannot display your position on a representation of an up-to-date airspace map. A dedicated mapping GPS can do this.

If at all possible get one with a colour screen, as it will make reading an airspace map easier. Because these types of devices are typically intended for use in the outdoors, they usually come with screens that, while small, are quite readable in bright sunlight.

Examples of this type of device include the Garmin GPSMap 60 and 76 series (Note the inclusion of the word MAP in the product name is crucial – the GPS 60 is a different and much less useful device) and the Satmap Active 10.

The Garmin models are particularly popular because regularly updated UK airspace maps in Garmin-ready format are available free online (see the final section for web links).

The combination of a screen you can read in sunlight, compatibility with up-to-date airspace maps and battery life measured in dozens of hours makes these a popular choice.

There is a device available called the Aware GPS, which shows your position directly on the 1:500,000 airspace chart. The chart can be updated for free, monthly, and the device is endorsed by the National Air Traffic Services. It has a bright, readable touchscreen and is easy to use. Its biggest disadvantage for paraglider pilots is its poor battery life. Out of the box, fully charged it's good for only one hour's operation at full brightness. This can be extended by three hours with the available battery pack. This may be OK for your first few flights XC, but the last thing you want is to be four hours into your greatest ever flight, over a part of the country you've never even driven through before, and have your mapping GPS battery fail, forcing you to land or risk infringing airspace.

PDAS/PNAS

PDAs (Personal Digital Assistants) are small touchscreen pocket computers running operating systems such as PalmOS or Windows CE. Examples include the Hewlett Packard iPAQ range. They were somewhat popular in the early 2000s, but most of their functionality has been taken over by smartphones, which means PDAs can be picked up online second hand reasonably cheaply.

PNAs (personal navigation assistants) are simply portable in-car satnavs.

LK8000 is a free, open source "tactical flight computer", a piece of software that you can download and install onto a range of PDAs and PNAs. It features moving map indications, audible alarms as you're approaching airspace boundaries, and many other features too numerous to list.

The advantage of LK8000 over dedicated mapping GPSs is that it is free, designed specifically for aviation use and works "out of the box" on cheap hardware.

Disadvantages are mainly about power consumption and readability. Whatever hardware you choose, you will most likely need to use an external battery pack. This is an extra bit of preparation you'll need to do, plus some additional wires and connections to deal with – nothing you can't easily fit in a cockpit. Also, the most common issue with LK8000 is finding a device whose screen is readable outdoors. I've seen some top expert pilots flying with big sunshades over their instrument pods. This suggests firstly that even the most dedicated pilots haven't found a solution to the problem of readability, and secondly that they consider LK8000 worth the hassle.

XCSoar is an alternative to LK8000 compatible with PocketPC computers and Android phones.

PHONES WITH APPS

While a GPS equipped smartphone may seem to be the ideal platform for paragliding instrumentation, the reality in my experience is that there are few if any apps that are of direct use to the pilot in flight.

Beware of mobile phone or portable computer apps that purport to be varios. Phones don't (at the time of writing) have pressure transducer hardware. They calculate their altitudes from the accelerometers and the GPS hardware, and GPS is not and never will be much good for accurate altitudes. Phone app "varios" are therefore slow to react, inaccurate and misleading, to the point of being worse than useless. Vario apps are a programming exercise and a novelty toy, not a usable alternative to a proper instrument.

A later section deals with apps of interest to the pilot on the ground, of which there are many. For now, my advice is switch your smartphone to silent and stow it somewhere safe but reachable – if your landing doesn't go well, you want to be able to reach it with the minimum of fuss and be certain it's still in the pocket where you left it.

Paragliding is photogenic, cameras are getting cheaper, and online social media make sharing your experiences fun and easy.

There isn't space here to discuss still photography in detail, beyond saying that if you're going to take a camera with you when flying, above all make sure you secure it to yourself or your other equipment. Dropping a camera from height is illegal, dangerous and expensive. Don't do it.

Also, I repeat my previous advice about instrument fixation. You are a pilot first, photographer a distant second. Never let your attention be drawn into framing the perfect shot at the expense of maintaining a safe heading.

Filming moving images in flight used to be the preserve of professionals, people with thousands to spend on equipment, neck muscles of steel to support the weight of the camera and its batteries, and endless hours and specialist gear and skills to edit the tapes that were the result

Nowadays one can buy a high-definition video camera the size and weight of a pack of cigarettes for less than the cheapest vario. You can shoot for three or four hours on one battery charge and one memory stick, edit the footage on a bottom-of-the-range PC using free software and in a matter of minutes publish it to the web and share it with the world.

Sounds like common sense, but bears saying: never do anything in flight simply because someone – you or another person – has pointed a camera at you. The temptation to show off can be great. Resist it.

113

Any advice I could offer about which specific camera to use would most likely be out of date before I'd finished typing it, so the buying advice that follows is generic and aimed at the novice pilot/cameraman.

It is perfectly possible to photograph and video record your flights using "normal" cameras. The results, however, are likely to be relatively disappointing, for a number of reasons. Normal cameras typically have relatively restricted fields of view, which is fine for taking portraits or snapshots of landmarks or whatever you're pointing the camera directly at. In an action sport, however, you want to capture as much of what you can see as possible, and this means using a really wide angle lens. You will see some distortion at the edges of the picture, but a slightly distorted bit of footage of something crucial is far better than knowing it was happening just out of frame.

"Normal" cameras also often come with a plethora of features and settings for use at night, indoors, burst mode, speed settings, aperture settings, timers, etc. For flying, the ideal camera has two controls – power on/off, and start/stop recording. Any settings around frame rate or resolution can be part of your preparation – on the hill or in flight you should need to press no more than two buttons, and ideally be able to hear some confirmation that the button has indeed been pressed.

A dedicated action camera will cope far better than a normal camera with difficult conditions such being pointed directly at the sun or being bashed around in your kit bag.

If your lens angle is wide enough, then pointing the camera roughly in the right direction is good enough. Check how wide the field of view is before you buy – 160 degrees or more is ideal.

It can be helpful to have an LCD screen showing what the camera can see – but bear in mind that this will also consume battery power, and you won't be able to see it while you're flying. It may be useful for reviewing stuff when you've landed, but you can after all do that back home. Fit a memory stick big enough, and there should never be any need to delete stuff while you're out.

Many action cameras come with waterproof housings. This is a selling point if you intend using your camera for surfing, diving, canoeing or similar, but waterproofness isn't necessary for paragliding – if it's raining, LAND!

It's possible to get really, really cheap video cameras about the size of your thumb. While the quality of the footage they shoot isn't great (at least at the time of writing) they offer the possibility of mounting a camera in places you wouldn't or couldn't put something larger or more expensive.

MOUNTING THE CAMERA

It's worth repeating the earlier safety advice about attaching cameras to helmets. Most camera mount sets will firmly attach the camera to your helmet with strong adhesive stickers. Do not use these. Helmet cams should by secured with Velcro, so that in the event that you get lines wrapped around the camera (either on the ground or in flight), the camera will readily rip free. You will of course have a lanyard attached to yourself or your equipment which will stop you losing it entirely.

The obvious place to mount the camera is on the top or the side of your helmet, to give a "pilot's eye view" of your flying experience. If you do this, bear in mind while flying that your head is now a camera. Watching back your first helmet-mount video will show you just how much and how fast you jerk your head around while flying normally. Don't stop doing that – you need to keep flying safe. But from time to time take the time to keep your head as still as possible, or to move it smoothly to follow the movement of another pilot or other target.

Do experiment with alternative places to fix the camera. Ideas include:

- In your lap or on your leg or boot looking up at you
- On the front of your chest strap or instrument pod pointing forward
- Secured to the end of a pole mounted to your harness pointing back toward you
- Secured to the centre or the wingtip leading edge of the wing looking down the lines at you
- Hanging down from the trailing edge secured by a couple of spare lines, pointing forward, mounted in a stabilising tube to work as a sort of "chase cam"

MAKING A FILM

Being able to see your helmet cam footage back after a flight will, the first time you do it, be fascinating for you. It will be quite a bit less so for your buddies, and for your non-flying acquaintances and relatives the novelty wears off pretty fast, often before the end of the very first video you show them.

You will need to learn to compose and to edit. Again, this book isn't a manual of film-making. There are plenty of those available. However, a few words are offered here to make your friends and relatives more inclined to view your efforts.

Keep it short. In today's fast moving, attention-deficient, tl;dr media world, nobody wants to watch ten minutes of you boating about your local ridge set to the sound of the wind in the microphone and the occasional muttered curse when you get a minor tip collapse. Pick an mp3 of a song you like that's three minutes long or less, and cut your footage ruthlessly to fit it. Mute the sound your camera recorded unless there's something notable to hear – the sound of a skylark singing on the wing, say. Stick a title page on the video to remind you when and where you shot it.

Shoot filler: don't just set up, switch on the camera, put your helmet on and fly. Three minutes of footage of your point of view in flight is not novel or particularly interesting. Make a film with a beginning, middle and end. The flying should be the *highlight* of your video, and possibly the majority of it, but never the only thing in it. It's easy to structure a paragliding video this way. "Beginning" is your preparation – waking up, weather checks, breakfast, the journey, the walk, the setup and takeoff. Anything that introduces the concept that you're about to do something cool and worth watching. "Middle" is obviously the flying itself. "End" could include landing, maybe some packing, and some post-flight action in the pub, campsite or hospital, depending on how well your day went.

Shoot more than you think you need. You can always edit it down later. You ***should*** edit it down later. When you're out on the hill, point your camera everywhere. This way, later on, when you're sitting in front of a PC, you'll have plenty of material to choose from. Be ruthless, and throw the vast majority of it away. Keep your shots short – unless you're

117

speedflying the Eiger, in general it's better to keep changing what the viewer is looking at every few seconds. Long, mostly samey shots with not very much happening will lose people's interest fast, so cut, cut, cut, if you can.

Get more than one point of view. If you can share footage with someone else who was shooting that day, do so. Mix and match footage of other people, footage of yourself, and pictures taken from your point of view.

Don't use special effects. Modern digital video editing packages let you easily apply all sorts of wacky special effects. Resist temptation and keep these to a tasteful minimum.

Consider the following, from the Encyclopedia Britannica's online entry on film editing: "Some directors shoot as little as three times as much as is required…" – and that's talking about films with scripts. Action videos' editing ratios are more like ten, twenty or a hundred to one. As long as your batteries are charged and your memory card big enough, you can't shoot too much stuff, but you really should throw most of it away. Share the best 2% of what you shot, and it'll give a good impression.

When editing, copy the files off your camera memory card to a hard drive and work on those copies – it'll work much faster that way. Back up the files, then delete them from the memory card, put it back in the camera, and put the camera on charge. This is your preparation for your next flight.

This section assumes you've followed the advice given earlier and have got yourself a basic GPS/vario combination instrument. What follows is some fairly generic advice on what you can do with it.

SETTING AUDIO

Out of the box, most varios will beep when you are going up, and boop when you're in sinking air. Somewhere in between, when you're in rising air but you're sinking slowly through it, they'll generally be quiet.

When you first fly with your instrument, simply switch it on and try not to look at it. Grow accustomed to the sound it makes, and learn to associate those sounds with the physical sensations you're experiencing.

You'll notice that when you're flying, the first clue you'll have that you're in lift is through the seat of your pants, and your vario will only start beeping a second or two later. The beep is confirmation of what you already think you know. Note, however, that going from zero lift to 1m/s up feels exactly like going from 1.5m/s second down to 0.5m/s down – but only in the first case will you get a beep from the vario.

Once you've flown a few times with the sounds on and got used to NOT looking at the instrument, you can set the thresholds where the beeps and boops cut in and out, and how fast they get higher and faster as your climb rate increases. It's largely a matter of taste whether you do this and where you set the thresholds.

On the one hand, if you're flying along in reasonable ridge lift the gentle beep-beep-beep can be a reassuring noise, and when the instrument falls silent as you gently sink out you can concentrate on top-landing or side landing.

On the other, once you're away from the ridge, every additional bit of information you can gather about what's going on around you will help you stay up and go further. The dead zone in your vario's audio response between zero and something like 2m/s downwards is a zone where you're learning nothing if you're not looking at your instrument – which is exactly what you don't want to be doing. Therefore, there is school of thought that recommends setting your vario so that it beeps all the time, so that you can, without ever looking at it, instantly tell if your situation is improving or deteriorating, even slightly.

SETTING ALTIMETERS

We all remember the three kinds of altitude from our textbooks, don't we? QFH, QE2 and QPR, wasn't it?

The advantage with GPS/varios is that, after enough time to establish a good GPS lock, all these altimeters can set themselves. All you then need to know is which one you should be looking at. Before you use it for the first time, you should make sure your altimeters are reading out in feet.

I have trouble remembering which altimeter is which. My vario can display any two of three, and I always have them in the same order, so rather than having to remember which precise Q code is which, I keep it simple and deal with either altimeter one, two or three.

Furthermore, I simplify how I think of them, reducing their textbook definitions to the words "standard", "real", and "here".

"Standard" is the pressure altitude. Even on basic varios without GPS it never needs setting because it's referenced to a standard air pressure. If you're flying well inside an area where the airspace ceiling is quoted as "FL55" or similar, this is the altimeter you should be looking at. This is always my altimeter number 1.

"Real" is the actual altitude you're at above sea level, QNH. This needs setting every time you fly because the air pressure changes from day to day. If you bought a vario without GPS, you'd have to find out what height above sea level you were at when standing at takeoff, and enter that value, or worse still a pressure, into the instrument at the beginning of every flying day. Because you were smart and bought GPS, the instrument will spot how high you are and enter the value for you. If you're flying in an area where the airspace ceiling is given as 3500' or similar, this is the altimeter you should be looking at. This is always my altimeter number 2.

"Here" is the reference altitude, and is always altimeter 3 on my instrument. For ridge soaring, it's takeoff height, or if I don't bother to zero it before I launch, more accurately it's the height my instrument was at when it got a GPS lock, which is near enough. For a day at the ridge, it can stay there – you can use it to judge when and whether to run back to the ridge for a top up of height, or whether you're going to make the landing field with reference to where you took off, or just for the satisfaction of knowing you got a certain number of hundreds of feet above take off.

If you manage to make it to cloudbase, you've usually left the hill behind and are no longer interested in height above takeoff – you should be mainly looking at altimeter 1 or 2 depending on your airspace issues. On most instruments you can zero the "here" altimeter at any time, and doing so at cloudbase gives a good indication of how you're doing when you're going XC. Even if you're not Father Dougal, up high and all alone it can be very difficult to tell the difference between a cloud that is small, and a cloud that is far away. If you're climbing towards a cloud it's very useful to know that it's just a little one and you're going to "hit" it in the next 100 feet or so, not a monster that's a couple of thousand feet above you.

REFINDING LIFT

Even basic GPS varios will help you refind lift, or as they sometimes call it, pinpoint the last thermal.

At their simplest, every few seconds they save a data point which includes your position and climb rate. If you stop climbing, they will note your direction of travel and indicate to you, either graphically or with bearings and distances, where you were when you were last going up.

There is no guarantee, of course, that if you go back to that point that there will still be lift there – it's good, but it's not magic. Nevertheless, most days it is good enough that it feels almost like cheating. It is worth checking the manual for your instrument to set up the "last thermal" finder properly. It's no use having it set up so that it will direct you back to the last 4m/s thermal you were in – you might go months between finding one. I've got mine set for 0.5m/s, which at a ridge is mostly pointless but once in the flatlands is highly useful.

It's probably reasonable to say that few of us originally started paragliding with the idea of entering competitions. We may have been aware of the inevitability that if something moves someone, somewhere will race it, but it's hardly ever the primary motivation for getting into the sport.

That said, there is nothing like a little friendly competition to improve your flying.

Paragliding competition can be conveniently separated into four entirely different categories:

- Acro flying
- Landing accuracy
- Task-based racing
- Cross country leagues

Acro flying is very much experts-only territory and very far outside the scope of this book. Landing accuracy is less extreme but bears about as much resemblance to the average pilot's flying day as dressage does to pony trekking. These two disciplines will therefore not be discussed further.

TASK-BASED RACING

A group of pilots gathered at the same place on the same day are briefed on a task. The task generally consists of flying from a defined point, perhaps after a defined start time, via one or more waypoints to a defined goal, possibly dozens or hundreds of kilometres distant. The pilot who gets to goal first or fastest wins. Winning requires not just a fast, high performance wing, but also a great deal of tactical knowledge

123

and experience, and at the top level the courage to push the wing to the limits of its performance.

Start, finish and any interim waypoints are defined as cylinders of a specific radius centred on given sets of coordinates. In the old days, pilots would prove they'd flown to a waypoint by taking a photo from the air. Nowadays, of course, all scoring is done by GPS tracklog. Many GPSs will generate a specific type of file, the IGC file, which is coded in a way which prevents tampering with the contents of the file. Most dedicated flying instruments and many multifunctional instruments are capable of generating a full 3D IGC file – make sure you buy one that does. Serious competitors carry two such instruments in case one fails.

Task based comps are typically divided into categories to separate pilots flying the top level, high performance wings from lesser mortals on EN Cs and relative beginners on EN B wings.

The primary event for UK based newbie comp pilots is the BP Cup. This has over many years appeared in many formats, but has generally been held over a number of rounds in different areas of the country, with scores accumulated over the year before a final winner is declared. It offers an excellent grounding in the essentials of comp flying.

The Lakes Charity Classic event held in the Lake District in June runs competitions and coaching sessions as part of the larger event, and welcomes complete beginners to competition flying.

The British Club Challenge is a series of events focused on "fun and team flying" rather than "out and out racing", and it primarily gets entries from clubs in the more southern parts of the UK (at least since 2010).

Competition introduces a whole new set of skills to learn and challenges to overcome, and will therefore almost inevitably improve your all-round flying ability.

Even if you don't get involved in organised competition, you can sit down with a map, or Google Earth, and identify some goal points near, or perhaps not so near, to your home site. Learn to program them into your GPS, learn how to fly to them, know when you've made it, and make it to the next one. It will make your flying at your local site more interesting and challenging. Ask one of your local coaches to set you an achievable task for your home site.

CROSS COUNTRY LEAGUES

The most popular competition in the UK going by numbers alone is the UK XC league, with over 200 pilots participating in the national league and many more in clubs leagues each year. This is probably because it's cheap or free to enter, can't be cancelled by the weather, and doesn't require you to travel away from your home area if you don't want to.

There is no fixed venue or date – you are responsible for knowing when and where to fly. Your score is calculated from your six best flights of the year, but you can enter as many times as you like. For this reason, those people in the upper regions of the league are not only expert pilots flying high performance wings – they're also crucially expert meteorologists with the free time to fly whenever and wherever the weather is best. They also have the organisation and preparation skills to make it to the best flying sites on a given day with their gear and themselves set up for flights that could carry them over a hundred miles across the country navigating under, over and around controlled airspace.

Back in the real world, you can start by entering your local club league table with any flight over five kilometres. You're allowed three turnpoints within that, so you don't have to fly anything like five kilometres in a straight line.

If you can take off, fly 1300 metres down a ridge or dune and back, then do it again without landing in between, you've got an XC league qualifying flight right there... and you don't even have to hitchhike back to your car! But be warned – once you and a buddy or two start submitting flights, friendly competition can become addictive.

FLIGHT ANALYSIS

Once you've uploaded a flight to the XC League, you can analyse it in detail, play back through it point by recorded point, and generally see what went well and where you made mistakes. Once you start doing this, you can start to identify the limitations on your flights, and work on sorting them out.

What's even better is that you can do this exact same analysis on *all the other pilots' flights* too, not just from this year but from previous years. Look at the cross country flights that have been done from your home hill(s). Consider the following:

- What time of day did they take off?
- Where did they take off? Is it your usual launch point or somewhere different?
- How long did they fly for before they got the climb that took them away from the ridge?

- How high did they get in that first climb, compared to how high they'd got previously; in other words, what was their "go height", the altitude at which they stopped trying to stay at the hill and committed to going XC?
- What direction did they fly in when they first left the hill? How about later?
- What easily identifiable landmarks did they pass over or near?
- What maximum height did they reach, and how long did they stay at that height, and how many separate times did they get near that height (i.e. how many climbs did they do?)

Don't necessarily examine the flights of people who did huge distances. Chances are they're on wings of far higher performance than your own. Instead, look at XCs done by people flying EN A or EN B wings. If they can do these flights – so can you.

A full discussion of XC flying is well beyond the scope of this book, but your preparation to go XC should include some time spent in advance getting to know the ground downwind of where you intend to fly from, its landmarks and features, and the historically reliable routes for flying over it. These are the routes you'll be following. When you first find yourself away from the hill, five thousand feet up, it can be enormously comforting to be looking down at a landscape you recognise from your homework and thinking "the lift line is usually THAT way…" It's far preferable to just bumbling up over the back and wondering where to head next with no real idea.

You don't need an encyclopaedic knowledge of where you're going – just a really, really big landmark like a big road junction, reservoir or odd-shaped forest every five kilometres or so. You mental map for your first planned XC might be something like "get high over the back, stay slightly south of the next ridge, cross the motorway north of the wind turbine, follow the river, don't fly north of the massive roundabout by the industrial estate." Having that plan in your mind in advance will save you a lot of mental effort when you come to actually try it. Obviously your plan must be fluid – there's no point flying blindly along your predetermined track if one of your landmarks has a big blue hole over it. But at least you won't get lost.

HOW TO SCORE IN THE CROSS COUNTRY LEAGUE

Ultimately, big scores in the cross country league come from flying big distances. There's no way round this fact. The REALLY big scores come from flying big distances between two or round three points you've declared in advance. A little more on declares shortly.

But even as a beginner you can do a scoring flight. For the local club leagues you need only 5km, and for the national league 10km, to score. At my home site it's possible on the right day to fly a turnpoint flight that scores over 12km without ever leaving ridge lift, and you get to land by your car. Seasoned XC hounds will scoff, but it's all valuable practice and not necessarily as easy as it may seem, especially for the inexperienced. Apart from anything else, it gives you practice in the vital skills of making sure your GPS is working, the batteries are charged, you've uploaded it to your PC correctly, uploaded it to the website correctly etc. It is better to prepare well, and to have your failures and learn your lessons early, on your short flights, than to have them bite you when you've set a personal best. So treat every flight as a potential league-qualifying XC.

In the first instance, therefore, as a beginner, your mission is to fly a turnpoint flight.

Your first turnpoint flight:

Landing

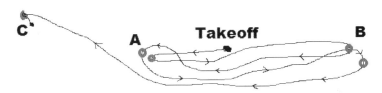

From takeoff, you must first fly towards where you intend to land. You should fly as far as you can while still keeping enough height and staying close enough to the lift to fly back past takeoff. When you've gone as far as you dare, turn, and fly back. You've just rounded turnpoint A. Top up your height if you need to in the reliable ridge lift where you launched.

Now fly as far as you can get away from A, ideally along a straight line from the landing field. Get as far as possible, but make sure again that you've enough height, and there's enough lift, to get you back to the takeoff. Make your turn at B.

Now fly back to A – even a little past it if you dare. This exercise is all about pushing the limits of how far you can fly. Don't put yourself in a dangerous position, but do risk bombing out and having to land safely and walk back up – it's all part of the learning curve. Get back to B, and again, if you can fly a little further on your second go, good for you.

Now, with your turnpoints in the bag, head for the landing field. Head, specifically, for the furthest corner of the landing field. If you arrive over it with plenty of height and you've checked it's not too windy, fly *past* the landing field, then back into it. Every additional 100 metres you can put onto the flight will count towards your score. The score is calculated as the distance A-B-A-B-C. Takeoff and landing points don't matter. You should be easily able to complete a flight to this plan over 5km long.

There are bonus multipliers available for flights that are harder than simply getting high and going as far as you can. Details can be found on the XC League website, but briefly they break down into:

- Circuit flights. Flights where you fly from A to B (and maybe C) and back to A. You score the total distance A-B-C, times a multiplier that depends on how hard it is to do that kind of flight. You can do quite a small circuit flight and submit it to the club league.
  When you submit a circuit flight, you have to tell the XC league software which specific datapoints within your IGC tracklog it should use as your turnpoints. You can find out which are the best ones by analysing your flight using GPSDump. See the "Online resources" section later for how to do this.
- Declared flights. This is where you define a start point and an end point and possible points between, and declare in advance by email or text message your intention to fly between them. Declared flight minimum distances are significant, but on the right day achievable for the well prepared beginner.

*Personal lesson: a declared flight is an excellent exercise in planning. You must identify a start cylinder near your home hill, and what you believe to be an achievable goal at least 25km away. You must program these two waypoints into your GPS and compile them into a route to be flown, so that you will know for certain when you have made it into the start and finish cylinders. You must learn the protocol for declaring a flight, and follow it to the letter. You must understand what the weather conditions must be like for your goal to be achievable, and must be able to get to the hill when these conditions arise. And then, of course, you must execute the flight, and make it to your goal. I believed I had done all these things. I made my declared goal cylinder with mere metres to spare, and was elated when the GPS blipped to let me know I had done so. I was elated for the hours it took to get home. I was elated right up to the point I uploaded the flight to the league, and realised I'd declared two cylinders which **measured from their centres** were 25.6 kilometres apart. You don't measure from the* *centres, you measure from the edges of the 400m radius cylinders. I had, therefore, declared (and successfully flown) 24.8km, just 200 metres short of the required minimum. It is a mistake I shall make only once.*

If you intend declaring a flight, one of the things you need to do is establish the distance between your turnpoints. There's a free PC program you can download off the internet that will allow you to precisely calculate the distance between any two points you define. The web address for download is given in the "Resources" section at the end of the book.

LEONARDO AND LIVE TRACKING

There is an alternative international XC league called Leonardo, the Global Flight Database. The scoring system there is slightly different from and more generous than that in the UK XC league. It offers similar opportunities for flight analysis after the event, including being able to download a 3D tracklog you can view in Google Earth.

Leonardo is also connected with Livetrack24, a website where you can watch, online, other people's paragliding flights as they happen. This is often used to make world-standard paragliding races, which can take place over dozens or hundreds of kilometres, workable as something like a spectator sport, as you can follow the race second by second in 3D on your computer screen, and see where all the competitors are relative to the turnpoints.

You don't need specialist kit to be livetracked – any smartphone can transmit your GPS position to the webserver

132

from a free app, and anyone can follow you from any web-connected PC. You don't even need a smartphone – a cheap Bluetooth GPS unit (which can be got for £10 or less) and an older phone will do the job, coverage permitting.

Leonardo is not widely used in the UK, but if you're going abroad to fly it may be worth investigating as a source for information on flights possible in the area you're visiting. Prepare, prepare, prepare.

A few personal thoughts about the business of getting back after an XC.

If one of your buddies goes over the back, and they're on a radio, wish them luck. If you can, offer to come and get them wherever they end up, or agree in advance that if one of you does get away, the other will run retrieve. This achieves a few things.

First of all, it's good karma. As paragliders we're a fairly self-reliant bunch most of the time, but when we've gone XC we can become dependent on the kindness of others to make it back to our cars and homes. Be a hero when you can, and others will repay you when it's your turn.

Secondly, there are few things more calculated to let a pilot relax and settle down to concentrate on their flying than the knowledge that their buddy is rooting for them and more importantly coming to get them. Removing any uncertainty about how to get back will improve performance, especially on your first few XCs.

Thirdly, while you're driving back, you can pretty much guarantee your passenger will be talking. They will be buzzed from their achievement, and it will be as fresh in their memory as it will ever be. They have just done what you hope to do. They have just flown a route that worked, seen the landmarks, found the climbs, spotted the landing field. You can learn more from them on the drive back than you can from any book (even this one), and their lessons will be tailored to your home site.

If two or more of you are aspiring to learn to go XC, seriously consider getting organised and prepare by stashing a car somewhere downwind of your home site, with the keys suitably hidden nearby so whoever gets there can get back. Again, the security of knowing there's a guarantee of transport back helps cut that psychological umbilical cord to the hill.

If you have a smartphone, install Google Latitude, and make sure all your friends do too. Once, you might have had to call your mate's mobile and describe where you thought you were based on your reading of the paper map you had, and try to guide them to where you were waiting. Now, if you can get to somewhere you've got cellular coverage, you can simply check in on Google Latitude, and all the people you've got on your friends list can find out where you are, on a map, to within a few metres, instantly. They can even get directions to you. As a retrieve tool, it's little short of magic. It's available for Android and iOS, and it's free.

Offer to be a retrieve driver for your local experts. On the one hand, you might find you spend a fair while driving to get them. On the other, if they're the kind of people who regularly fly 100km or more, if you're on the same hill as them you've a good chance that it's the best hill in the country that day. Plus, as you're driving back with them, you can grill them for information.

If you have to get yourself somewhere, be prepared to hitchhike. Have a sign for hitchhiking. It conveys the idea that you're not some chancer who doesn't have a car, you've a legitimate reason for needing a lift.

Take off your sunglasses and hat and make eye contact with drivers.

Carry your helmet in your hand – it marks you out as something other than a "normal" hitchhiker.

Smile.

Try not to have a beard – it really will affect your chances of a lift.

Try to stand somewhere that makes it easy for drivers to pull over. Find a layby, petrol station, bus stop etc, and stand a few metres away from it.

If you can find a petrol station, where drivers have already stopped and exited their cars, approach them directly. This has a far better hit rate than standing at the side of the road with your thumb out, plus there's somewhere dry and warm to wait that has food and drink.

Finally, if someone does pull over and offer you a lift and it strikes you as in any way dodgy, don't get in, even if you've been waiting ages. There's always another lift.

Paragliding is getting easier. Pilots are flying further and in greater numbers than ever before. This is partly down to the improvements in the design of wings, but it is also down to the incredible array of tools we now have at our disposal for weather prediction, pre-flight planning, post-flight analysis and communication.

Given the ever-changing nature of the internet, there's no way this list can possibly be comprehensive. It's a starting point, though. You can find live versions of all these links, plus others that may be added later, at the website for this book, www.preparetofly.co.uk .

http://www.bhpa.co.uk/ : Start here, especially if you're not yet CP rated. Lists schools and clubs, compiles and reports incident stats, advice on equipment and safety, Pilot and Advanced Pilot ratings, coaching courses, insurance and much more.

http://www.xcweather.co.uk/ : Extremely simple to understand and pretty reliable live weather map. Not a lot of detail, but very good for getting the bigger picture quickly in terms of wind strength and direction. Helps if your local site is reasonably close to one of the arrows.

http://rasp.inn.leedsmet.ac.uk/RASPtableGM8/RASPtableGM.html : xcweather on steroids. An excellent predictor of how usable the weather is actually going to be for paragliding and other soaring aircraft. Harder to use, but if you take the time to learn to use it, it can be incredibly accurate and comprehensive. Doesn't just do windspeed but covers a huge range of parameters to do with atmospheric stability generally. Once you start thinking of going XC, this will become one of your go-to sites.

http://rasp.stratus.org.uk/app/rasptable.php : RASP Stratus, an alternative server for the same data with slightly different display parameters available. Try both.

http://www.sat24.com/gb Realtime satellite imagery giving an excellent impression of the current weather pattern.

http://www.facebook.com/ : Share your photos and videos, reminisce about the day's exploits, speculate on the next day's weather, plan an expedition, even arrange a retrieve if you're running the app from your phone.

https://twitter.com/ : can be a useful tool for communicating weather conditions and where you're going to be flying, but its usefulness is directly proportional to how many other people you know use it, and how much they use it.

http://www.youtube.com/ : endless source of entertainment and information. Try not to watch *too* many videos of people crashing. They can be legitimately instructive, though. Get an account for free and get your own videos up there.

https://vimeo.com/ : an alternative to Youtube, if you want or need it. A good source of instruction on how to make better videos.

http://www.xcleague.com/xc/ : upload your flights here, and see how yours compare to your mates' scores. Then analyse their flights and those of the experts to see how you can improve.

http://www.paraglidingforum.com/ : when it's raining or windy or dark, go here and shoot the breeze with the like-minded, or pick their brains. Hints, tips, news, discussions, jokes, rumours, arguments, advice, classified ads, reviews, all of it on just one subject but with contributors from around the world, all conversing in (mostly) good English. Hosts links to Leonardo and other useful tools.

http://www.paraglidingearth.com/pgearth/index.php?pays =75 : crazy-comprehensive attempt at a paragliding site guide for the entire planet complete with live weather reports showing whether it's flyable at your site of choice right now.

http://www.paraglidingmap.com/NewFeatures.aspx : smartphone app that puts paragliding earth in your pocket.

http://www.mrsoft.fi/ohj02en.htm : homepage for WGS84 calculator, a free, tiny app for your PC that will allow you to measure the distance between any two points on the globe. I wish I'd downloaded this about a week earlier than I did...

https://www.google.com/latitude/b/0/ : like a magic arrow appearing over your head saying "Here I am!" to all your friends. If someone needs to find you, make sure you both have this on your smartphones.

http://tinyurl.com/bq4ka4m : OS Grid Converter, an iOS app that converts in either direction between British OSGrid references (used on the maps and by some, but not all, GPSs) and WGS84 Lat/Long coordinates (used by all GPSs). Very useful to have at a comp briefing, but beware – it's not always accurate! (Bitter experience...) Can also give your current position in both sets of coordinate systems.

http://www.expandingknowledge.com/Jerome/PG/Main.ht m : a mine of information, not all of it entirely up-to-date but still very good, especially the tips page
http://www.expandingknowledge.com/Jerome/PG/Skill/All /J_Tips/English.htm

http://www.gethome.no/stein.sorensen/body_gpsdump.htm : GPS dump, the simplest, most comprehensive bit of software for getting your flights off your GPS and onto your PC. Free. Worth having and learning to use as a backup/alternative even if your instrument came with its own package. In particular, will allow you to identify which specific data points in an IGC file are the ones you need to specify are your turn points for your optimum triangle or out and return flight.

Open the relevant IGC file, do Edit/Select All, then Misc/OLC/OLC Statistics (use selected pos.). The program will show the data point number, time, and exact location for all the turn points on the optimum turn point flight, triangle and out and return your flight might represent.

http://www.lk8000.it/ : LK8000, a free open source flight computer for certain car satnavs and various other GPS enabled pocket computers.

http://www.xcsoar.org/ : a free open source flight computer for PocketPCs and Android.

http://xcplanner.appspot.com/ : excellent tool for planning XC flights, and in particular for viewing airspace boundaries for various levels on your PC screen.

http://ukgarminairmap.wikispaces.com/ : free airspace maps compatible with Garmin mapping GPS units.

http://www.ebay.co.uk/ : excellent source of cheap decades-old deathtrap paragliders for Darwin Award candidates who want to teach themselves to fly. Also a good place to get Chinese import electronics including radios and headsets.

http://www.skyads.eu/ Free classified advertising service for paragliders, hang-gliders and other free-flyers.

http://www.pilotnotes.me.uk/ : A set of hyperlinked crib notes to help you get through the BHPA Pilot Rating written exam.

http://www.penninesoaringclub.org.uk/index.php/penninelibrary/swatting : three PDFs of crib notes for the Pilot exam that you can print out and read in the bath.

http://tinyurl.com/bonnegz :somewhere to buy airspace maps from. Don't waste your time and money, and confuse yourself, by buying 1:250,000 versions. You'll find there are airspaces shown on your mapping GPS that aren't on there. Get the proper maps, the half mil ones, which show *all* the boundaries.

Personal lesson: when preparing to fly XC, you could fold your airmap such that it fits in a mapcase with your starting point at the bottom and your general direction of travel pointing up. OR you could prepare further in advance... Scan the map into a graphics program on your PC, and create a cropped and rotated custom map at A4 for every site you use regularly. Make it double sided so that when you fly off the edge you

A few magazine and online articles about thermalling and similar...(note: the availability of these sites cannot be guaranteed)

http://www.ojovolador.com/eng/read/tecnics/thermal_flying/thermal_flying.htm

http://www.xcmag.com/2010/08/essential-selection-the-core/

http://xtc-paragliding.com/articles/thermallingP1.html (part one of three)

http://www.bpcup.co.uk/thermalling.php (a competition rule page, but good advice for thermalling generally.

http://tinyurl.com/ctz8k73 : quite an old article on XC flying (it mentions the author's performance in the '95 season!) but still worth reading.

BOOKS & DVDS

While the internet is a huge and ever-growing source of excellent information and free things, it's still worth building a small library of books and DVDs to turn to when the nights are dark and you're square eyed from the PC monitor. There are quite a few "learn to fly" style books about, especially in second hand bookshops. There is a great deal of overlap in their content, making it pointless to own more than one or two, so if you get the best ones first you can ignore the rest.

I have no commercial connection with any of the following products, beyond being a satisfied customer of them all. It's worth saying that earlier editions of some of the books below will be available second hand – don't buy them. They're regularly updated to take account of developments in equipment and techniques, so buy the latest edition. Paragliding equipment is still developing and changing fast enough that a ten year old book is usually seriously out of date in at least some of its details.

BHPA Pilot's Handbook, by Mark Dale: the official textbook of paragliding. Contains everything you need to know to pass your written exams for Pilot and Advanced Pilot ratings.

Touching Cloudbase: A complete guide to paragliding, by Ian Currer. An good alternative text for beginners and developing pilots. Covers a lot of the same material as that found in the Pilot's Handbook, but in a slightly more informal style and with many colour photographs and diagrams.

Thermal Flying, by Burkhard Martens: a beautifully produced full colour hardcover book full of good information on how to find and stay in thermals. Somewhat biased towards European big mountain flying conditions where they have huge, reliable, strong thermals, but still worth owning, especially if you ever intend flying abroad.

50k or Bust!, by Nigel Page: excellent, no nonsense advice on flying cross country in specifically British conditions, aimed at the recently qualified novice, i.e. you! Profusely illustrated with diagrams and photographs. Everyone who wants to get away from the ridge should have this book. Available via http://tinyurl.com/cd7htlu

Pilot's Weather, by Brian Cosgrove: for successful paragliding, you need to be obsessed with the weather. This is one of the best books available for learning about it.

Speed to Fly & Security in Flight: two excellent DVDs in one package, covering cross country flying and SIV.

Performance Flying: an extension of the information in the previous two films. All three highly recommended, available from any paragliding equipment dealer or http://www.escapexc.com/dvds/

Paragliding Ground Handling Techniques: not an ambiguous title for this DVD. The importance of practicing ground handling cannot be overstated. You need to spend as much time as you can practicing ground handling, and watching this DVD will help.

29575741R00086

Printed in Great Britain
by Amazon